OVERLOOK ILLUSTRATED LIVES:

Ayn Rand

Jeff Britting was associate producer of the documentary
film *Ayn Rand: A Sense of Life*, which was nominated for an
Academy Award for best documentary. Since 1998 he has
been archivist at the Ayn Rand Institute in Irvine, California.

Ayn Rand

Jeff Britting

OVERLOOK DUCKWORTH

NEW YORK • WOODSTOCK • LONDON

First published in the United States in 2004 by
Overlook Duckworth, Peter Mayer Publishers, Inc.
New York, Woodstock, and London

NEW YORK:
141 Wooster Street
New York, NY 10012

WOODSTOCK:
One Overlook Drive
Woodstock, NY 12498
www.overlookpress.com
[For individual orders, bulk and special sales, contact our Woodstock office]

LONDON:
Gerald Duckworth & Co. Ltd.
90-93 Cowcross Street
London EC1M 6BF
www.ducknet.co.uk

Cataloging-in-Publication Data is available from the Library of Congress

Type formatting and layout by Bernard Schleifer Company
Printed in Singapore
ISBN 1-58567-406-0 (US)
ISBN 0-7156-3269-8 (UK)
9 8 7 6 5 4 3 2 1

Contents

Acknowledgments

This brief biography of Ayn Rand is based on archival materials that have been my research and preservation focus for eleven years. I began working with Ayn Rand's papers in 1993, while making a documentary film about her life (*Ayn Rand: A Sense of Life,* Strand Releasing, 1997). After the film's release, I became archivist at the Ayn Rand Institute, managing her personal papers and the acquisition of related collections.

I would like to thank Dr. Leonard Peikoff, for generously making available Ayn Rand's published works and unpublished papers for this book, which I have prepared without his review.

I would also like to thank my editors at The Overlook Press, Tracy Carns and David Mulrooney, as well as Arnold Dolin.

The following individuals and organizations deserve thanks for their support, comments, research, and other assistance: Dr. Yaron Brook, Dr. Judith Berliner, Scott McConnell, Doug Johnsonson, Chris Patrouch, Kevin King, Doug Rose, Anu Seppala, Dr. Dina Garmong, Dr. Shoshana Milgram, Richard Ralston, Dr. Harry Binswanger, Michael Paxton, Dr. Robert Mayhew, Dr. Allan Gotthelf, Betsy Speicher, James S. Valliant, Sharyn Blumenthal, Dr. Merrill Schleier, Noel Palomo-Lovinski, Arline Mann, Dwyane Hicks, Alex Lebedev, Mrs. Archibald Ogden, June Kurisu, Daniel Greene, Jeff Burch, Julius Shulman, Steve Smith, Cynthia Peikoff, Debi Ghate, Roxanne Mayweather (SearchWorks), Terry Thiele (Luna Imaging), Marc Baer, Ben Bayer, Simon Federman, Donna Montrezza, Julie Repass, Larry Benson, Marilee Dragsdahl, and Mark Chapman.

Special thanks are extended to the patrons of the Ayn Rand Institute: their support has made the Institute's archival program possible; and to Dr. Michael S. Berliner, whose clear thought, good counsel, and editorial advice made this book possible.

A postcard from Rand's family:
the Stock Exchange, St. Petersburg

Looking Out
1905–1914

> Petrograd was not born; it was created. The will of man
> raised it where men did not choose to settle. . . . An
> implacable emperor commanded into being the city and the
> ground under the city. . . . Nature makes mistakes and takes
> chances; it mixes its colors and knows little of straight lines.
> But Petrograd is the work of man who knows what he wants
> . . . [The city] has no legend, no folklore; it is not glorified in
> nameless songs down nameless roads . . . Petrograd does
> not need a soul; it has a mind.
>
> Ayn Rand, *We the Living*

In her first published novel, Ayn Rand paid tribute to the city of
her birth, St. Petersburg, developing a theme that would become
a focus of her mature writing—the exaltation of the individual
mind and its power to command nature in the service of human
life. At the time of her birth, on February 2, 1905, the city of
imposing Tsarist palaces and broad squares, erected over a
swamp and delegated by Peter the Great to be Russia's window
on western Europe, was convulsed in a panic, as the first
sparks of revolution had flared. Throughout the year of Rand's
birth, the events that came to symbolize the revolution—Bloody
Sunday in St. Petersburg, the *Potemkin* mutiny and massacre
in Odessa, strikes and riots across the country—set the stage for
the adoption, more than a decade later, of a form of government
whose underlying philosophy Rand would repeatedly condemn
throughout her career.

The building at 47/21 Klinsky Pereulok (now 40/27 Zabalkansky Blvd.), where the Rosenbaums lived when Rand was born

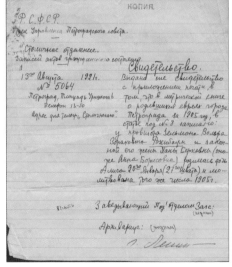

A section of Rand's birth certificate, identifying her birthday as January 20 (before Russia adopted the Gregorian calendar)

Rand's high estimation of St. Petersburg did not extend to the rest of Russia, however. Even in her youth, she considered her homeland an "accidental cesspool of civilization" and its inhabitants "mystical, stupid, backward, and sentimental."[1] In the cultured, upper-middle-class environment in which Alisa Zinovyevna Rosenbaum was raised (she didn't adopt the name Ayn Rand until her arrival in the United States in her early twenties), "real life and real intelligence and real people" were to be sought exclusively in the West.

Her father, Zinovy Zacharovich Rosenbaum, had surmounted most of pre-revolutionary Russia's obstacles to success. In spite of quotas restricting the admittance of Jews into universities, he obtained a degree in chemistry, financed by working his way through school. He was also able to subsidize the university education of his eight siblings and, after he moved to St. Petersburg, became the co-proprietor of a successful pharmacy. At the peak of his prosperity, Zinovy Zacharovich owned the building on Nevsky Prospekt, overlooking Znamenskaya (later renamed Vosstaniya) Square, in which both his pharmacy and the large family apartment were located.

Anna Borisovna Rosenbaum, Rand's mother, was the daughter of a successful Petersburg tailor, Boris Kaplan. Regarded as the family's intellectual, Anna Borisovna had a wide variety of interests in cultural affairs and current events. The family apartment was the setting for numerous gatherings of her large, extended family of Petersburg professionals and their children.

Though Anna Borisovna and Zinovy Zacharovich were of Jewish background, he was agnostic and she was only nominally observant. (Though they ate matzoh during Passover, a Christmas tree decorated the apartment in winter.) Unpublished correspondence suggests that both parents respected logic and purposefulness and considered individualism a virtue: "Each person," wrote Rand's mother, "is the maker of his own happiness," "the architect of his own fortune." Both parents regarded education as important.

Rand's two younger sisters excelled in the arts. Natalia, known as Natasha (born in 1907) studied at the St. Petersburg Conservatory and became an accomplished pianist. Eleanora, known as Nora (born in 1910), aspired to a career in the fine arts.

Rand's early childhood relationship with her father was respectfully affectionate, though distant. In fact, Zinovy Zacharovich had few dealings with the children. She later recalled that "children's education was totally in the hands of the mother . . . therefore, father never interfered, and there was no such thing as him exercising any influence over us."

In later years, Rand remembered Anna Borisovna as a conscientious and attentive mother, though she was often irritable and her resentment of child rearing was sometimes apparent.

Rand with her doll, on the knee of her father, Zinovy Zacharovich, ca. 1907

Mother and daughter had contentious, frequently antagonistic, disputes.

My big clashes with Mother in childhood were [due to] the fact that I was anti-social, as she would call it. She always demanded that I be more interested in other children. Why didn't I like to play with others? Why didn't I have any girlfriends? That was kind of the nagging refrain. She did not make my life miserable with it. To do her justice, she never enforced it nor made it sound like a serious reproach.

Rand described her earliest approach to life as being an "enormous series" of questions aimed at understanding the things around her. She referred to the act of focusing on "the unusual" as a personal "leitmotif." She taught herself to read at the age of six, and it was at this age that a growing awareness of her environment took hold, a curiosity that soon blossomed though lessons in violin, piano, drawing, and foreign languages.

Left: *Anna Borisovna Rosenbaum, ca. 1913*

Right: *The Rosenbaum family on holiday, ca. 1912. Rand is second from the left.*

Because of this curiosity, her "social development" was less important to her than her intellectual development. She had particular antipathy for unchosen social and familial obligations: "I didn't like being attached to a family. . . . I resented enormously any implication that anything to do with the family was binding on me."

Even at an early age, her predominant interest was literature. In order to get Rand started in the study of French, Anna Borisovna subscribed her to a French children's magazine. The first story she read, concerning a helpless orphan boy and his kindly godmother, left her with a feeling of bored contempt. However, the second story, a detective adventure in which an adult solves a mystery through the employment of logic, was a revelation. It wasn't so much the mystery and suspense of the tale, but the fact that the protagonist's actions conveyed purpose, ambition, and ability—qualities Rand always found attractive. The story enabled her to relive the experience: instead of merely observing admirable qualities in others, she could now retain them in a tangible form and re-experience them whenever she wished by simply recalling the story. She began seeking similar stories and soon began writing her own.

In 1913, at the age of eight, Rand attended St. Petersburg's first motion picture exhibitions and, fascinated by the action-oriented silent films, she began writing scenarios. Noting her daughter's interest in action stories, Anna Borisovna subscribed Rand to a French boy's magazine that featured adventure serials, which was to result in another discovery: Maurice Champagne's *La Vallée Mystérieuse* (*The Mysterious Valley*), a Rudyard Kipling-style adventure set in India.

The Mysterious Valley: *illustration of Cyrus Paltons by René Giffey.*

The wildly extravagant plot featured British soldiers assaulted by a tiger manipulated by an evil rajah opposed to British rule. But the real attraction to Rand was the story's main character, Cyrus Paltons, who, when captured and threatened with torture, defiantly opposes the rajah. The story's descriptions and illustrations of Paltons crystallized Rand's vision of her male ideal. She was, as she later recalled, a young girl in love. Paltons's tall, svelte physique was later embodied in the protagonists, both male and female, of Rand's mature novels.

With the exploits of Cyrus Paltons and *The Mysterious Valley* fresh in her mind, the nine-year-old Rand that summer found her own adventures, as well as a girlish love interest in a long-legged young boy, in Switzerland, where the Rosenbaums' vacation ended abruptly with Germany's declaration of war. With England the only open avenue back to Russia, the family spent a week in London awaiting steamship passage to St. Petersburg.

It was during this time of upheaval and anxiety that Rand was struck by the idea that writing would be the defining passion of her life and the career she would pursue as an adult. As she passed through the London streets in the company of her parents, a poster for a musical revue grabbed her attention; its illustration of a troupe of dance-hall girls with pageboy haircuts set her imagination to work. By that evening, she had created a series of adventures inspired by these colorful dancers, and as her sisters listened intently to her story, the thought struck her that storytelling was an adult profession. When the moment passed, she realized her future was set:

> *I remember the day and the hour. I did not start by trying to describe the folks next door—but by inventing people who did things the folks next door would never do. I could summon no interest or enthusiasm for "people as they are"—when I had in my mind a blinding picture of people as they could be.*[2]

At the end of an exhausting week, the Rosenbaums boarded a ship to St. Petersburg, newly renamed Petrograd. Unable to obtain a first-class cabin, the family slept on tables in the ship's

The Matterhorn; part of Rand's collection of "Pictures I Like"

dining room. The trip was an anxious one for Anna Borisovna, as the ship traversed a North Sea terrorized by German U-Boats; but Rand found the trip exciting—her impromptu decision to become a writer had become a solemn conviction that an important future lay before her.

Nora, Rand, and Natasha, ca. 1914

The Stoyunina Gymnasium, where
Rand attended elementary school.
Her only girlfriend among her
classmates was a sister of Vladimir
Nabokov.

Important Things
1915–1925

Having arrived safely in Petrograd after their precarious trip home, the Rosenbaums resumed their lives amid the tumult of a country at war. Rand, now nine years old, was enrolled in school. She anticipated that formal education would be an entrée into the world of adults, an opportunity to learn and meet peers who shared her interest in ideas. Though she excelled academically, with rare exceptions school was a disappointment. Motivated by a strong belief in the future that awaited her as an author and intellectual, she routinely proceeded at a faster pace than her fellow students, and she often grew bored and resentful of her instructors.

She was similarly frustrated in her hope to find like-minded fellow students with whom she could share her deepest concerns. She made an observation at the time which reflected this disappointment and revealed an aspect of herself that stood in the way of success in the social sphere:

> *I [was] very proud of my essence but not of my form. . . . I was bashful, alternating between bashfulness and violence. If and when there would be any occasion [after the age of twelve] of any discussion of principles or of asserting myself in the realm of ideas, I would be too violent. I would get too angry. And I was aware that it isn't right, [but] I had no other form of behavior.*

She considered her form a "technical flaw" of childhood, one she would have to overcome as she matured.

Restless in school, she secretly began writing novels in class. These short, dry, synopsis-like works indicated her longing for adulthood and contained fantastic projections of adult interests. One novel, which she later recalled in detail, was about an English girl seeking to enlist in her country's war against Germany. Though rejected at first because of her gender and her age, she persuades the authorities to allow her into the army. She eventually rescues her country from invasion by establishing a machine gun position on an English beach and single-handedly defeating the landing German army.

Rand's early novels were written effortlessly, without any awareness of the conventions of plot structure, characterization, or style. However, what is readily apparent is the focus on individuality, goal-orientation, and a fascination with heroism:

I had absolutely no literary concepts. I didn't know that there were rules or that it was called "plot". . . . [In] the kind of stories that bored me . . . there was no progression. . . . The idea that the story had to have a plot was to me synonymous with a story.

In *The Romantic Manifesto*, an expression of Rand's mature thought, she defined plot structure as a "purposeful progression of logically connected events leading to the resolution of a climax." This, in many ways, can be seen as an outgrowth of the stories she wrote from her youth: from an interest in actual purposeful men and women, she would develop "purpose" into a literary technique, one that became a hallmark of her mature fiction.

Although access to newspapers was forbidden by her parents, Rand began reading them in secret. During her first year in school, she read an article by an educator who asserted that children acquire their moral values in school and nowhere else. Rand reacted with characteristic indignation. Was she not defining her own ideals and presenting them in her stories? She vowed to compose a rebuttal, thereby to confirm her belief that "the world of ideas is my business, that I should answer this woman—she's wrong."

S. Solomko's The Temptation.
*Undated postcard, part of Rand's
collection of "Pictures I Like"*

As her formal education
continued, she was intro-
duced to Russian literature,
much of which—with its
themes of dark tragedy and
unfulfilled romance—she
found uncongenial to her
literary ideals. Nevertheless,
she studied and wrote
essays on the poetry of
Pushkin and plays of
Shakespeare, always receiving excellent grades. When
the opportunity arose, she
enthusiastically wrote compositions expressing her
own views on literature,
but nothing in her studies could rival the significance of Cyrus
Paltons, whose heroic character was Rand's love and emotional
preoccupation until at least the age of twelve.

In February 1917, the Russian Revolution began and the same
year, Rand recalled, another revolution occurred in her thinking,
one setting the stage for her future development as a philosopher.
Alongside her curiosity about the world and her pursuit of
"favorites," a new type of question arose within her. She began
asking *why* she liked what she did, and, as a result, she began
integrating her ideas into wider generalizations. She called this
approach to integrating ideas "thinking in principle." Rand recorded
her views in a diary and analyzed why they were important and on
what evidence they were based. She thereby combined "thinking
in principle" with what she called "going by reason." The topics
she covered in her diary included some of the traditional problems

of philosophy (a concept she was still too young to fully grasp), among them freedom and individualism, the relationship between reason and freedom, and the value of freedom for the heroic individual. She termed these "important things."

Throughout 1917, as Russia was torn apart by revolution, Rand followed the events with an eager curiosity. Her journal writing from this period exhibited the immediacy of a first-hand witness. For the first time in her life, she experienced an adult-like connection with the newspaper headlines of the present:

> The house where we lived at that time was on a big public square, and this was in February 1917, and the first thing we saw was this mob gathering and filling the entire square. And I still remember it . . . a complete sea of faces and the first red banners. . . . And then the second day there were some armed police or Cossacks that appeared and they were ordering the people to put down the banners. And the crowd refused. . . . The third day, the people were not on the square, but fighting began in the streets. And what I saw was that on the corner of the square and the street branching off from it there were lines of soldiers shooting down the street.

Rand continued to follow the political events throughout early 1917. The abdication of the Tsar, the formation of the Provisional Government under Kerensky, the cessation of war with Germany, and the promise of free elections dominated public discussion. "To me it seemed to be the fight for freedom. . . . And by freedom, at that age, I would already have meant individualism. That it's man who is free, in the singular. . . . And therefore I thought it was wonderful. It was almost like fiction taking place in reality. And Kerensky became my great hero at that time."

In the summer of 1917 the Rosenbaums vacationed at Terijoki, a Finnish seaside resort, and it was one of the happiest summers of Rand's childhood. However, that October, the Bolshevik Party maneuvered into position, Lenin returned from exile, and the Provisional Government was consigned to, in Trotsky's famous words, "the dustbin of history."

For Rand, the Communist motto, "from each according to his ability, to each according to his needs," meant that man should live

Above *Approximate view from the Rosenbaums' apartment windows in their building facing Znamenskaya Square at 120 Nevsky Prospekt*

Left *Znamenskaya Square in 1917. The Rosenbaums' apartment is on the left.*

for the state and not his own personal happiness. The revolution was her first confrontation with the "ethics of altruism" (the view that service to others is the highest moral virtue), which she rejected instantly as an attack on men of "intelligence, ability, and heroism." During the civil war that ensued, Petrograd's population was reduced by two-thirds, due to the starvation and flight of its citizens from revolutionary terror. The Rosenbaum family felt an immediate impact,

Eugène Legenisel's Victor Hugo, Adolescent. *19th century. Part of Rand's collection of "Pictures I Like"*

as Zinovy Zacharovich's building, and the pharmacy contained therein, was nationalized and sealed. The underlying cause of these events, she had concluded, was the ethics of altruism.

Despite the chaos, in early 1918 Rand—now thirteen years old—found a refuge from her misery in the inspiring works of French novelist Victor Hugo. "I discovered Victor Hugo," she wrote in 1962, "when I was thirteen, in the stifling, sordid ugliness of Soviet Russia. One would have to have lived on some pestilent planet in order to fully understand what his novels—and his radiant universe—meant to me then." She was enthralled by the grandeur and moral courage of Hugo's characters, which he presented in dramatic, luminous prose. Reading him, she said, was like "entering a cathedral."[1] Rand had already begun imagining her future as a Russian writer living abroad, important enough, like Hugo, to be translated into the world's languages.

During this same period, Rand made the following entry in her journal: "Today I decided to be an atheist." "I remember making that entry," she later said, "as if it were an integration of something that had been growing for a long time." She reasoned that if "God is perfect and man can never be that perfect, the idea necessarily makes man low and imperfect and places something above him," and thus it is "degrading to man." This again foreshadows a theme of Rand's mature thought—the issue of reason *versus* mysticism and the connection of the issue to human values. "Just as religion has preempted the field of ethics, turning morality *against* man, so it has usurped the highest moral concepts of our language, placing them outside this earth and beyond man's reach."[2] To Rand, the commitment to atheism was a consequence of an overall commitment to reason: "[I]f something cannot be proved by reason, then it's nonsense. . . . I can't name [a time] when it was different. That was a chronic *leitmotif.*"

The Rosenbaums left Petrograd in the fall of 1918, moving south to the Crimea to escape the fighting. Prudently, Zinovy Zacharovich had secretly stockpiled cash and hidden his wife's jewelry in the months preceding the October Revolution. Russians with similar means began fleeing the country, but refusing to believe that Communism could last, he was determined to reclaim his building and business in Petrograd. The decision not to evacuate his family turned out to be a costly mistake. During the Russian Civil War (1918–21), the Rosenbaums settled in the Crimean town of Yevpatoria, where Rand attended high school. Her father operated a private pharmacy, which he would lose and reestablish as control of the Crimea alternated between the Reds and Whites. With the Red victory in 1921, the value of Zinovy Zacharovich's currency savings was reduced to nothing.

During high school, Rand read all the available works of Hugo and Edmond Rostand, as well as novels by Alexandre Dumas and Walter Scott. She remained desperate to find a peer with whom she could discuss ideas, but her Crimean classmates kept their distance.

Occasionally, fellow students asked Rand, who had a reputation as an excellent student, to tutor them or help with homework. Rand discovered that she enjoyed the process of breaking down complex issues and explaining the answers.

Throughout Rand's high school years, the Crimean school system operated under pre-Soviet standards. Accordingly, she was introduced to the American political

Bust of Aristotle; part of Rand's collection of "Pictures I Like"

system of individual rights and—through an elementary primer on logic—to Aristotle and syllogistic logic, particularly the concept of *consistency*, which, she recalled, made an enormous impression on her. "It's one of the few instances where I know reading a specific thing had an influence on me—as if a light bulb went off in my mind."

With political discussion occurring just about everywhere, Rand found common ground during the Crimean period with her father, who shared her views on freedom and individualism. "I began to be very friendly with my father because we were the only two in the family seriously interested in current politics from a standpoint of anti-Communism and on principle." She began referring openly to her goal of becoming a writer. While her mother merely "tolerated" the decision, her father "approved very highly."

At the end of the civil war, the Rosenbaums returned north to pick up the pieces that remained of their former life. Her diary had

Rand (bottom, far left) with her graduating class at High School no. 4 in Yevpatoria, Crimea

grown in length: "I wrote all kinds of anti-Soviet things in it and I continued it when we were in the Crimea and burned it all when we were coming back to Petrograd." Such was the concern for safety and the necessity to conceal dissent, even in the writings of a teenager.

The Rosenbaums passed through Moscow en route to Petrograd. After years in a small Crimean town, experiencing the vastness of Moscow produced an epiphany:

> *I remember standing on a square. . . . And it suddenly struck me. . . . "How enormous it is, and how many people, and it's just one city". . . . I suddenly had the concrete sense of how many large cities there were in the world—and I had to address all of them. All of those numbers had to hear of me, and of what I was going to say. And the feeling was marvelously solemn.*

Leningrad State University (center)

Rand's university application photograph and the second-floor terrace of the university

Right *Rand, ca. 1924, dressed for a party*

Upon their return to Petrograd, the Rosenbaums reclaimed but a single room of their former apartment and commercial building. Zinovy Zacharovich obtained work in a private cooperative pharmacy, and Anna Borisovna began translating books and teaching. On the verge of adulthood, Rand confronted both a ruined city and her immediate future.

In 1921, at the age of sixteen, she enrolled in Petrograd State University as a history major. She selected history in order to acquire a factual understanding of man's development, with a concentration on medieval Europe, because it presented a "stylized," completely un-Soviet subject matter. She also studied philosophy, in order to achieve an objective definition of her values. Since the pro-

fessors lectured mainly from their own published writings, she spent most of her time
at home studying these texts, attending only
the special seminars. Her twenty-six courses
included history of Ancient Greece, history
of Socialism, and seminars in 16th-century
England and 17th-century France. Rand's experience with philosophy was mixed: she was
quick to reject anything with the merest hint
of obscurity and mysticism. For example, she
favored Aristotle, "the arch realist and the
advocate of the validity of man's mind," over
Plato. Another major discovery was Nietzsche.
Incited by her cousin, Vera Guzarchik, who
claimed that Nietzsche had "beat me to all
of my ideas," Rand eagerly read *Thus Spoke
Zarathustra*, embracing Nietzsche's exaltation
of the exceptional individual. But her enthusiasm diminished while reading his attack on
rationality in *The Birth of Tragedy*. Rand's two

*Lev Bekkerman, Rand's first adult
romantic interest, and the model for
the character Leo in* We the Living.
*Bekkerman was executed by the NKVD
in 1937, a fact Rand never learned*

major literary discoveries of the period were Schiller, whose plays
she admired for their grand, heroic scale, and Dostoevsky, whose
novels integrated moral evaluations and masterful plot structures.

A greater personal discovery was what she called the "tremen-
dous sense of life transfusion" of Viennese and French operettas.
With productions mounted for the first time since the revolution,
she attended Carl Millöcker's *Der Bettelstudent* (*The Beggar Student*),
which she saw eleven times, as well as operettas by Emmerich
Kálmán and Jacques Offenbach. "[Operetta] was my first great art
passion. That really saved my life. . . . It was the most marvelous
benevolent universe." One production, a new work by Franz Lehár,
incorporated both contemporary dress and a European skyline, her
most vivid experience yet of a non-Soviet world.

Eventually, cinema, particularly German and American films,
supplanted operetta as a source of personal joy and her window
to the West. Films such as *Das Indische Grabmal* (*The Indian*

Tomb), directed by Joe May, the works of Fritz Lang, and the contemporary dramas of Cecil B. DeMille were "a much more specific, not merely symbolic view of life abroad. . . . And I remember there were some American movies where you could see New York, just shots, usually long shots, and I would sit through two shows just to catch it . . . it seemed completely incredible."

These cinematic glimpses of New York were the source of Rand's commitment to one day celebrate the skyscraper as a symbol of man's achievement.

Despite her abhorrence of Russia and the increasing dreariness of Soviet life, she maintained a positive view. In later letters, Anna Borisovna recalled that Rand considered negative things unimportant and put much more weight on success than on failure. This

Right *C. B. Balashov as Simon Rymanowicz in* Der Bettelstudent, *autographed in 1923*

Below *Nevsky Prospekt, near one of the operetta theaters Rand afforded by walking to the university, thereby saving the streetcar fares*

Conrad Veidt, Rand's favorite silent screen star

attitude anticipated her "benevolent universe" premise, her adult view that happiness and success on earth are normal and possible.

Conditions at Petrograd State University were similar to the fictitious "Technological Institute" of *We the Living*. A small number of Communist cells operated within the larger anti-Communist student body and, at first, meetings and debate between both groups occurred openly, but near the end of Rand's second year, the Soviet government ordered a purge of students with anti-revolutionary backgrounds. Non-proletarians, Rand among them, were expelled, and the anti-Communist student leaders were arrested. However, a visiting delegation of Western scientists protested the expulsions. Bowing to foreign pressure, the Soviet government reinstated non-proletarian students with a remaining year of coursework, and Rand was able to resume her education.

Rand finished her coursework in 1924 and graduated with honors, her transition into young adulthood now complete. She had studied philosophy, but—with the exception of Aristotle—found it unhelpful in defining her values. The philosophy she sought was not in the university, but was a growing body of knowledge within her—a philosophy of which the first written glimmers had begun to appear in her diary seven years earlier.

While she attended university, Rand set aside the half-finished literary projects she started as a teenager and temporarily stopped writing fiction. She did continue to plan and outline future novels and plays, the themes of which were almost invariably individualism and political freedom, with events either set in the past or projected into the future. The circumstances of the present—when the present consisted of avoiding lice-infested tramway passengers, or procuring butter with a doctor's prescription, or going hungry—did not inspire her to write heroic fiction. Nevertheless, Rand could not be discouraged. She enrolled at the State Technicum for Screen Arts, a film school established by Lenin for the development of Soviet cinema. Her objective was to study screenwriting, and in preparation she also began writing film reviews and short essays on Hollywood, some of which were published. She briefly thought about becoming a Soviet screenwriter, subtly incorporating her ethical and political ideas into her scripts. As an experiment, she

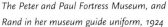

The Peter and Paul Fortress Museum, and
Rand in her museum guide uniform, 1924

Above *Rand's student "passbook" at the State Technicum for Screen Arts, 1924–25*

Left *Building on Tchaikovsky St. in Petrograd that housed the State Technicum for Screen Arts*

presented a fellow film student—
a good Soviet citizen—with a
writing sample that employed
this technique. Immediately the
student became unnerved, sensing
something odd about its theme,
so much so that Rand concluded
that there was no future for her in
Soviet cinema—or in Soviet society:
"I would have been probably
dead within one year," she later
concluded.

In a 1927 letter recounting this period, Anna Borisovna recalled the hours Rand spent in her bedroom, yelling in despair. There was no breathing space in Russia for dissidents. Rand's vision of heroism and individualism was impossible to reconcile with the collectivism envisioned by Lenin and the founders of the Soviet Union, and her bedroom door was no airtight defense against a police state intolerant of dissent.

Acting poses, while a student at the State Technicum for Screen Arts, 1924–25, where she also studied cinematography

This Borovikovsky studio photo (ca. 1924) of Rand was displayed in the window of his Petrograd studio.

Cover of "Hollywood: American
City of Movies," one of Rand's
Russian film publications.

Rand's Soviet passport, 1925

Freedom to Write
1926–1935

During the Russian Civil War, there were nearly three million casualties, and lines of communication between Russia and the West were interrupted. With the ending of the Civil War in 1921, communication was restored and emigrants were able to contact family members within Soviet Russia to assess their safety. In 1924 Anna Borisovna received such a letter from a cousin living in Chicago.

With the fear constantly in mind that Rand's vocalization of her frustration could put her in prison, Anna Borisovna—to Rand's eternal gratitude—proposed a visit to Chicago by her oldest daughter. The timing of this suggestion was fortunate: Lenin's "War Communism" had been replaced by the more liberal New Economic Policy (NEP), and travel restrictions for students wishing to study abroad had been temporarily eased. In addition, the Rosenbaums learned that their American relatives owned a theater exhibiting silent films. The official purpose of Rand's visit would be to study the film industry first-hand and then to return and contribute the fruits of this research toward the advancement of Soviet film. This stated purpose, however, was a ruse; Rand planned to make her American visit permanent, "crossing over the lake" (in the words of her mother) to Canada, if necessary, to avoid returning to Russia. Her goal was first to establish herself as a screenwriter, thereafter "graduating into literature"—as she would later put it in her 1936 unfinished "An Attempt at the Beginning of an Autobiography"—when her command of English had improved. She applied to the Soviet government for a passport.

During this period, the Rosenbaums had been adopting a series of increasingly bizarre strategies to assist Rand in realizing her ambition and to safeguard their own survival. Anna Borisovna joined the Communist Union of Educational Workers and worked as an instructor in a worker's school, thereby gaining proletarian status and helping to insure Rand's film school admittance and a job as a museum guide. Natasha and Nora pursued endless cycles of vocational education in various trades, while struggling to manifest sufficient "social commitment" at school. Yet, in the privacy of the Rosenbaum apartment, the letters and film magazines sent from American relatives and the preparations for Rand's departure sustained their hopes. The soon-to-depart Rand was nicknamed "the American resident"; a family cat was named "Los Angeles."

In late 1925, Rand received her Soviet passport. After selling some of Anna Borisovna's remaining jewelry to raise funds, her parents purchased the rail and steamship tickets from Leningrad to Chicago. On January 17, 1926, family and friends gathered to see her off at Moscow Station in Leningrad. Excerpts from several unpublished letters from those present describe the scene:

> [A] miserably cold Leningrad day, the terrible 17th, railroad station, railroad platform. . . . When you were standing on the balcony of the train and the train's commandant finally separated you from us, you looked so miniature, slim, young and pretty. . . . The second bell finally sounds and then the train whistle. You gradually disappear into the Leningrad darkness, the very last thing is your cry "stop running after the train"—and waving your hand.

As Anna Borisovna related in a letter to her daughter: "You loudly called out to us, 'By the time I return, I'll be famous.'" After the train departed, Zinovy Zacharovich exclaimed: "Just you wait, just you wait! Alisa will yet show the world who she is."

The trip from Leningrad to Chicago took more than five weeks. Arriving on February 19, 1926, in a New York harbor shrouded by heavy fog, Rand was unable to catch a glimpse of the Statue of Liberty; instead she fixed her sight on the luminous skyline, visible from the New York pier. As snow fell she started to cry what later were described as "tears of splendor."[1] Accompanying her, as she entered the United States, were the mental outlines of seventeen novels, screenplays, and plays.

Right *Rand (left) in Berlin with her cousin Vera Guzarchik, a medical student with whom she celebrated her 21st birthday, on her way to America*

Below *The* De Grasse, *the French liner on which Rand sailed to America, and her ticket stub for the passage*

LIGNE DE NEW-YORK   N° 18486

Mᵉˡˡᵉ ALICE ROSENBO M.

La présentation de ce Talon peut être requise en cour voyage et il devra être remis au débarquement à destination; à défaut, la Compagnie a exiger le prix du passage.

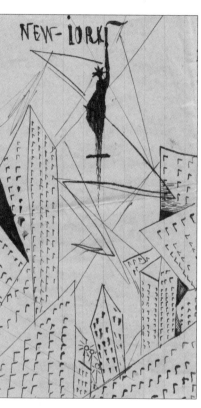

Left *Among the hundreds of Nora's drawings and paintings that she mailed to Rand—mostly fashion illustrations or depictions of Rands's adventures*

Right *Nora's 1926 drawing of New York and the Statue of Liberty. To Rand and her family, America was a "distant ideal." "Going to America . . . was literally for all of us somewhat like going to Mars."*

Upon her arrival in Chicago, Rand began writing film scenarios to submit to Hollywood producers. As her film diary attests, she attended the cinema almost daily. Her scripts were written in Russian, and then translated and polished by a younger cousin into "proper English." The content was similar to that of her earlier stories: utterly fantastic projections, among which figured a noble crook equipped with a parachute to leap from skyscrapers. The sound of her typewriter clacking late into the night often kept relatives awake.

A new country, language, and profession raised the issue of adopting a new name. Vocal in her opposition to the Bolsheviks and confident of one day achieving fame in the United States, she was mindful of the price her family might pay for her outspokenness. While still in Russia—a letter from her sister reveals—she picked "Rand" as her new surname and considered "Lil" as a possible first name. Ultimately, she selected "Ayn," which she derived from a Finnish name. In August 1926, Ayn Rand—or Alice, as she was listed on official documents—renewed her visa for six months. Borrowing $100 from relatives for a trip to California, she arrived in Los Angeles with a letter of introduction from a Chicago film distributor addressed to the public relations department at Cecil B. DeMille's production company. DeMille's spectacular, plot-oriented dramas had captivated her, and "Cecil B. DeMille" had been one of her many nicknames in Russia.

On September 3, 1926, Rand registered at the Hollywood Studio Club, a Y.W.C.A. residence for young women employed in the film industry. The following day, she took a bus to DeMille's Culver City studios and presented her letter of introduction to the studio's publicity department. She was granted a courtesy interview, but as

The Portnoy and Satrin families, relatives of Anna Borisovna Rosenbaum, who were primarily responsible for bringing Rand to America. She lived with both the Satrins and Goldbergs in Chicago from February to August 1926.

Rand's unmailed June 18, 1927, postcard of Cecil B. DeMille's Hollywood residence. On the reverse, she wrote in English to her parents: ". . . am sending this to say that I am perfectly alright, very much so. Am very happy with my work and scenarios. P.S. That's the house I saw when I was driving with C.B. DeMille, as I wrote you in my last letter."[1]

Cecil B. DeMille's handwritten pass to the backlot of The King of Kings, September 13, 1926: "DeMille Studios. Sept. 13. Pass Miss Rand to my set good all week. C.B. DeMille."

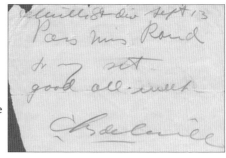

expected, no writing jobs were available. Rand left the meeting and walked out the studio's front entrance and onto the driveway, where a large roadster sat idling. Its driver was Cecil B. DeMille.

> He drives up to the gate, stops, looks at me, and asks, "Why are you looking at me?". . . . Apparently he had noticed me before. So I told him I had just come from Russia and I am very happy to see him. So he opens the door of the car and says, "Get in." I didn't know where we were going; I got in and he started driving. . . . I told him that I want to be a writer and he was my favorite director. And my English was atrocious. . . . Where he was driving was the back lot. They were shooting The King of Kings.

As they drove onto the set of *The King of Kings*, with its magnificent recreation of New Testament Jerusalem, DeMille advised her that if she wanted to write for films, she must learn how movies are made, and during breaks in the afternoon's shooting, he explained some of the filmmaking process to her. By the end of the day, he had written her a pass for another visit to the back lot. Soon thereafter, she was offered a job as an extra. She worked continuously for the next three months on *The King of Kings*, until principal photography was finished.

Rand also submitted scenarios during this time, but they were rejected by DeMille's story department as far-fetched. The story editor suggested that Rand write about more conventional characters, but instead of heeding this advice she viewed it as "the enemy" attitude, and continued writing as she pleased.

The King of Kings provided more than an income for Rand: on the set she met a young actor named Frank O'Connor, who would become her husband of fifty years. She had first encountered him in a streetcar on the way to the studio and was captivated immediately. She soon discovered his tall, quiet presence (a striking resemblance to the Cyrus Paltons character she had long idealized) on the set of *The King of Kings*, in which he was cast as a Roman soldier. Desperate to meet him, she blocked his path during the

Rand's pencil drawing of Frank O'Conner [sic] *in the Roman soldier uniform he wore as an extra in* The King of Kings. *She later described her first sight of him on the set: "He was magnificent. They had given him a very good antique costume. . . . It was a short tunic, with sandals laced up to his knees, and a big toga over it, with an embroidered collar, and some kind of . . . scarf tied around his face, with ends streaming down and a piece of embroidery in front. I later, from memory, drew a picture of him. . . . What I couldn't forget is the profile, the way he looked with that headdress."*

filming of a crowd sequence, and they finally spoke. To her great disappointment, it turned out to be his last day and she did not see "the DeMille extra" on the set again.

After filming on *The King of Kings* was completed, DeMille—who nicknamed Rand "Caviar"—offered her an entry-level position as a junior screenwriter in his story department, and she began researching backgrounds for stories he had purchased and planned to produce. One day while waiting to interview a building foreman at a construction site in Hollywood, she unexpectedly ran into Frank O'Connor at a nearby library. Recognizing each other immediately, they renewed their acquaintance. On April 15, 1929, Ayn Rand and Frank O'Connor were married in a civil ceremony in downtown Los Angeles.

Rand left her job with DeMille Pictures in 1927 and worked sporadically at unskilled jobs to supplement the money she received from her parents. Shortly after her marriage, she obtained, through Ivan Lebedeff—an actor and fellow Russian émigré—a clerical job in the studio wardrobe department of RKO Radio Pictures, while Frank continued to work as a film extra and actor in small parts. She read extensively in both American and European literature in translation, improving her command of English as a result. During the next year and a half, she wrote several short stories in the style of O. Henry, including romantic adventures with triumphant

Rand with girls from Hollywood Studio Club on "Clean Up Hollywood Day," April 1927.

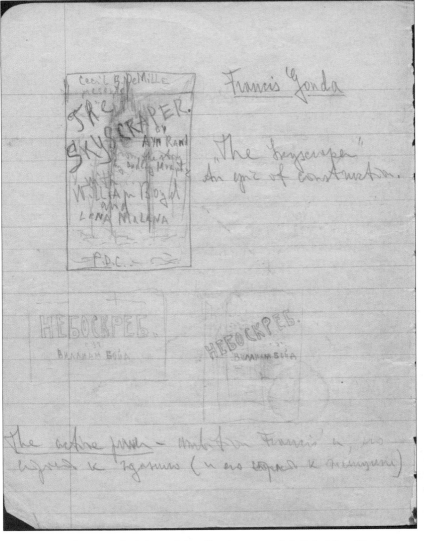

From Rand's 1927 notebook, her rendering of imaginary posters in both English and Russian for "Skyscraper" (1928), a project for DeMille. Among the other scenarios she worked on were three films produced by the studio: The Angel of Broadway (1927), His Dog (1927), and Craig's Wife (1928).

heroes. She also worked on the outline of a novel she was never to write entitled "The Little Street," the theme of which is the betrayal of the exceptional man and the enshrinement of mediocrity. Two distinct archetypes—the light-hearted action hero and the embittered idealist—would surface repeatedly in the screenplays and stories Rand wrote over the next eight years.

During this period, she wrote long letters, often forty pages or more, to her family about the important events in her life and the issues that troubled her. She also wrote sporadically in her journal, once giving herself the following advice:

> *The secret of life: You must be nothing but will. Know what you want and do it. Know what you are doing and why you are doing it, every minute of the day. All will and all control. Send everything else to hell!*[3]

By 1929 Ayn Rand was ready to attempt another major work in English. She soon began outlining a novel tentatively titled "Airtight"—later renamed *We the Living*—the theme of which she identified as "the supreme value of a human life and the evil of a totalitarian state that claims the right to sacrifice it."[4] The protagonist of the novel is a young engineering student, Kira Argounova, who feigns a love affair with an idealistic member of the Communist party in order to save her actual love, a self-destructive son of a

Right *Rand's green card, received June 29, 1929. She became a U.S. citizen on March 3, 1931.*

Facing page *Frank O'Connor, late 1920s. He appeared in numerous films, including* Cimarron *(1931) and both the film and stage versions of* As Husbands Go *(1933–34).*

Tsarist admiral. The inspiration for *We the Living* came from her concern for the sanctity of the individual, but the suggestion to write it came from Frank and his brother, Nick Carter, a newspaper reporter living in Los Angeles, who encouraged Rand to tell the world the truth about life in Soviet Russia. The other project she was working on at the time—a futuristic novel set in an orbiting space station—was shelved.

Although Rand felt she was not yet ready to write about the ideal man—a literary goal since childhood—this story about a young woman's attitude toward her unrealized ideal was quite within her grasp, and she thoroughly understood the background and psychology of her characters. She completed the outline quickly, but the actual writing progressed slowly. The opening chapter was revised numerous times, as Rand struggled to cast her thoughts into English prose. She composed the work in English, but also at times in Russian or French, which led to numerous errors in grammar, syntax, and style.

We the Living was a long-range assignment, often interrupted by shorter projects that could be completed quickly. Among these were several screenplays—some written in collaboration with another screenwriter, between 1930 to 1932, and "Red Pawn," a solo effort in which Rand aimed to expose the evil of dictatorship and equate Communism with religion. Like *We the Living*, the plot of "Red Pawn" involves a love triangle: a woman becomes the mistress of a Soviet prison commandant in order to secure the freedom of a prisoner she loves. The outline for the screenplay was brought to the attention of the story department of Universal Pictures, who bought it for $1,500 in 1932. It was Rand's first professional sale of an original work of fiction, and the money enabled her to quit her wardrobe job and work full-time on *We the Living*.

In an unpublished 1932 letter to her Chicago relatives, she described her life:

> *I've had a pretty hard time. However, I shouldn't complain . . . I did work in the wardrobe at R.K.O—for over three years. It was not a bad job—not sewing (for I still can't sew a stitch), but in the wardrobe office. I wasn't getting very much money—but enough to carry on. The*

work was quite hard—nerve wracking—a lot of details, a lot of rushes, excitement, and—quite frequently—a lot of overtime. Besides, I had to keep house—try to cook, and wash dishes, and such—at night. But I simply could not give up writing. I came to America to write—and I had not forgotten that. That's something I'll never give up. But it was pretty much of a problem—I didn't have very much time to write and when I did find an hour or two at night, I was so tired that I could hardly get any ideas, my head felt too heavy—and one can't do one's best work after hours and hours in a studio wardrobe (the messiest department of a studio). Sometimes, I got up at 5:30 or 6:00 am—to write a few hours before going to work. All this time I've been working on a novel—a real big novel I want to write—about Russia.

We the Living was completed in 1934. Through her Hollywood contacts, Rand acquired a New York agent, Jean Wick, who began submitting the book to major publishing houses. However, the reception was cool. In the intellectual community of mid-1930s New York, there was a widely held sympathy with Marxism and even the USSR.

Despite mounting rejections, the sale of "Red Pawn" gave Rand the financial freedom to write another new work, a play that would result in a major commercial success and her first taste of fame. In 1933, after attending a performance of the courtroom drama *The Trial of Mary Dugan*, Rand conceived of an idea for a play about a murder trial whose jury is selected from the audience each night. *Penthouse Legend*, as the play was originally titled, was meant to present evidence so evenly balanced that the verdict would depend entirely on the subconsciously held philosophical beliefs of the jury. On trial for murder was Karen Andre, a woman of passionate assertiveness. An innocent verdict would affirm the value of independence and what Rand called "your highest vision of yourself."[4] A guilty verdict would affirm the importance of conformity and conventional values. A different ending was written for each possible verdict.

Rand received two offers to produce the work: one from a modest Hollywood theatrical producer and well-known character actor, E. E. Clive; the other from an experienced Broadway producer,

A. H. Woods. She accepted Clive's offer because of his assurance that no script changes would be implemented without her approval. Although well directed, the production was a disturbing experience for her. "I found it nerve-wracking, day after day to hear people reading my lines and not knowing what they were saying." Re-titled *Woman on Trial*, the play opened on October 24, 1934. It had a short but successful run at the Hollywood Playhouse and received good reviews.

Meanwhile, efforts to produce "Red Pawn" had reached a dead end. Josef von Sternberg had been considering it as a vehicle for Marlene Dietrich, but after the commercial failure of *The Scarlet Empress*, his most recent film with Dietrich, he vowed never to direct another film set in Russia. Shortly afterwards, Rand wrote a novella, "Ideal," which served as an outlet for her contempt for Hollywood. The protagonist of "Ideal" is an actress—modeled on Greta Garbo—accused of murder and on the run from the police, who unsuccessfully seeks help from fans who had written her letters hypocritically expressing their adulation.

Late in 1934, A. H. Woods reinstated his offer to produce *Penthouse Legend,* which he retitled *Night of January 16th.* Rand's demand for final script approval was granted, though it was ambiguously worded in her contract, and Woods was granted an exclusive option on the theatrical rights. Nonetheless, she thought the play's Hollywood success gave her sufficient bargaining power to enforce her terms. In addition to enhancing her standing as a screenwriter, a Broadway production would provide an excuse to relocate to New York, a city she first saw displayed on a St. Petersburg motion picture screen and which attracted her above all others. It would also provide an opportunity to monitor the faltering effort of her agent to sell *We the Living*.

In late November 1934 Ayn Rand and Frank O'Connor moved to New York City. Simultaneously, A. H. Wood's funding for the Broadway production of *Night of January 16th* fell though. With Frank unable to find work, the option money was their only source of income. However, Rand hired a new, well-known agent, Ann Watkins, who was enthusiastic about the chances of finding a

Rand with unidentified woman at the Hollywood Playhouse, where Woman on Trial *opened October 22, 1934. "I don't remember the opening night. All I remember is the marquee. [E.E.] Clive put my name in lights. And so on the marquee there was 'Woman on Trial by Ayn Rand.' That gave me a thrill because that was the sort of idea I would have had in Russia: your name in lights. I had read that in American fan magazines." Marlene Dietrich attended the opening night party.*

publisher for *We the Living*. Watkins also found work for Rand as a reader hired on a freelance basis to evaluate the screen potential of novels for RKO and Metro-Goldwyn-Mayer studios.

Rand's time in New York was nevertheless a period of financial, creative, and personal strain. She began to plan her next novel, but her irregular employment made it impossible to work on any long-range writing: she could work only at research and writing "in small glances." While publishers continued to reject *We the Living*, she renewed her effort to bring her family to the United States, having begun earlier with her youngest sister, whom she had tried unsuccessfully to enroll in an American university. Despite their difficult situation in Russia, the Rosenbaums were overjoyed by reports of Rand's mounting successes. Through their letters they encouraged her with reactions to *Night of January 16th*.

From Rand's sister Nora:

> *Dact [a nickname for Ayn, short for Pterodactyl], dear, how well you wrote it, what good, idealistic and real people you've created. This is probably the essence of one's genius—to write a play in such a way that you are not indifferently reading about some fake heroes, but feel like you are right there with them, hating their enemies, who also seem to be, not fake, but real people.*

Although full of unsolicited advice about her daughter's eating and work habits, Anna Borisovna's letters were also a source of encouragement, especially during this period of financial and professional struggle: "It is not important," she wrote in a letter, "if your success is interrupted with stops. What *is* important is to be in love with life; to strongly believe in yourself; it *is* always important to remember that the road of great people is difficult and uneven." And she praised her daughter's "unbending decision to achieve her goal and unwavering pursuit of her chosen road in life. I am certain that had it not been for your self-assuredness, purposefulness and drive, you would have found yourself having to retreat in the face of seemingly impenetrable stupidity."

In late 1935 funding for *Night of January 16th* was secured and the play went into rehearsals. Rand fought bitterly with Woods over line changes and creative control. The play about a clash of moral values had devolved into a backstage clash between its producer and playwright. Rand ultimately distanced herself from what she felt had become a butchered work.

At the Broadway opening, she sat at the rear of the Ambassador Theatre, yawning in boredom. She seldom entered the theater again during its twenty-nine-week run. The experience surrounding *Night of January 16th* was a profound disappointment that forged in her an identification with the play's protagonist—the character on stage fighting for her life was not the only woman on trial.

Above *Rand's sister Nora with husband Feodor
(Fedya) Drobyshev, ca. 1934*

Left *Nora's romantic drawings had not been
welcomed by her Soviet teachers, similar to the
response of Irina's teachers in* We the Living:
*"They said my peasant women looked like cabaret
dancers and my workers were too graceful."*
*(*We the Living, *p. 256)*

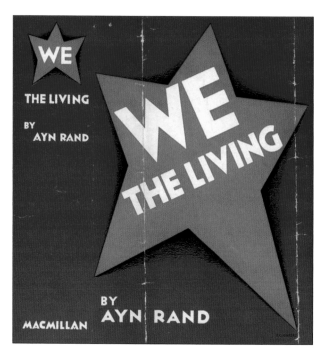

Left *Original Ekhenberg-designed dust jacket for* We the Living, *published by Macmillan in April 1936*

Below *One of Rand's practice inscriptions for a copy of* We the Living *dated April 4, 1936. Sarah Satrin had been married to Sol Lipsky, owner of the New Lyric movie theater in Chicago, in 1926, when Rand lived with them after her arrival from Russia.*

To Sarah Satrin

– with profound gratitude for saving me from the kind of hell described in this book –

Ayn

4 – 2 – 1936

The Ideal
1936–1942

In the mid-1930s, Rand began to closely follow American politics, and economics, about which she read widely in magazines and books. Although she had voted for Franklin Roosevelt in 1932 because he opposed Prohibition, by the time she arrived in New York she had come to the conclusion that he opposed economic freedom as well. In her view, as she later summarized it, liberals wanted intellectual freedom but not economic freedom, while conservatives wanted economic freedom but not intellectual freedom; both sides ignored the fact that the Declaration of Independence, with its fundamental affirmation of "life, liberty, and the pursuit of happiness," entails that "a free mind and a free market are corollaries."[1] America—Rand's haven from Soviet tyranny—did not understand what made it a haven.

In 1935 came some welcome news: while she was engaged in the arduous rewriting of *Night of January 16th*, Rand learned that Macmillan and Company had accepted *We the Living*. Macmillan's initial reaction to the novel was mixed. The editorial board was sharply divided: Granville Hicks, a member of the American Communist Party and editor of the left-wing journal *The New Masses*, was adamantly against the book, but his opinion was overruled by that of George P. Brett, Sr., board chairman of the publishing house, who authorized the publication. Rand's "Russian novel" would be published, and she would thereby fulfill the request made by a fellow Russian before her departure in 1926: "When you get out, tell the rest of the world we are dying here."[2]

In spring 1936 Macmillan published *We the Living* with a modest first printing of 3,000 copies. The press coverage included hundreds of short articles and 125 reviews, but despite the significant quantity, the author was generally displeased with the reviews, even the complimentary ones, for not adequately drawing attention to the philosophical ideas the novel dramatized. For her own part, Rand was very pleased with the plot and ideas, but noted some writing problems: occasional grammatical lapses and underwritten passages, and a style at times derivative of Victor Hugo.

Despite minimal advertising, the book's sales picked up gradually and began to find a strong readership through word of mouth. However, after requesting additional promotional copies from Macmillan, Rand was told that *We the Living* was out of print, a breach of its contractual obligation to keep the book in print for at least two years. Expecting only a modest reception for the book, Macmillan had set the book with type, which was destroyed shortly after publication, instead of engraving it on plates. *We the Living* would not reappear in print in the United States for another twenty-three years. Nevertheless, Rand had now found success as a writer in three different media, having written a film treatment for Hollywood, a successful play for Broadway, and her first novel.

```
FAVORITE RADIO PROGRAM - Midnight Jamboree, Mr. Suffens.  Station WEVD. NYC.

FAVORITE MOVIE STAR - Greta Garbo.

FAVORITE AUTHOR - Sinclair Lewis.

FAVORITE COLUMNIST - Menken.

FAVORITE COMPOSER - Emmerich Kalmann.

FAVORITE MOVIE DIRECTOR - Fritz Lang.

FAVORITE WOMAN NOVELIST - None.  Too sentimental, and even the best fail to go
                          into deeper things, and remain too typically feminine in style and
                          viewpoint.  Also dislike their extreme preoccupation with love.  Love
                          should have its place in any picture, but not be the whole picture.
```

Above *From the first page of a questionnaire Rand completed as part of Macmillan's publicity campaign for* We the Living

Right *One of a series of Pach Bros. studio portraits arranged by Macmillan for the publication of* We the Living, *1936*

Royalties from *Night of January 16th* were substantial, and in this period of financial security, her thoughts turned to a new novel, "Second-Hand Lives," later retitled *The Fountainhead*.

The idea for *The Fountainhead* grew out of an earlier experience in Hollywood. In her RKO days, before the sale of "Red Pawn," she had become acquainted with Marcella Bannert (later Rabwin), an ambitious young assistant to producer David O. Selznick. Bannert, a neighbor in Rand's apartment building, recommended "Red Pawn" to the agent who eventually sold the property to Universal Pictures. Rand was always grateful for her neighbor's help, but couldn't help observing that, while both she and Bannert were ambitious and committed to careers in the film industry, one as a writer and the other as a producer, they had completely opposite views regarding the importance of other people. For Rand, the opinions of others mattered only when such people shared her values; for Bannert, the opinions of others *were* her values. Rand remembered Bannert saying,

> *Here's what I want out of life. If nobody had an automobile, I would not want one. If automobiles exist and some people don't have them, I want an automobile. If some people have two automobiles, I want two automobiles.*

This is the basic conflict of *The Fountainhead*, the plot of which opposes two types of people: the egoist, the man of first-hand judgment, who uses his mind to guide his life; and the selfless man, the second-hander, who bases his life on the opinions of others. The novel is, among other things, a dramatization of the idea that self-sacrifice is, at root, the sacrifice of one's mind, of one's independent judgment. Howard Roark, the architect hero of *The Fountainhead*, summarizes this conflict:

> *[Second-handers] have no concern for facts, ideas, work. . . . They're concerned only with people. They don't ask: "Is it true?" They ask: "Is this what others think is true?" Not to judge, but to repeat. Not to do, but to give the impression of doing. Not creation, but show. Not ability, but friendship. Not merit, but pull. What would happen to the world without those who do, think, work, produce?*[3]

Rand's first note on *The Fountainhead*, dated December 4, 1935, is: "The first purpose of this book is a *defense of egoism in its real meaning*."[4] She later described the theme of *The Fountainhead* as "individualism *versus* collectivism, not in politics but in man's soul."[5]

In a reply to a 1943 fan letter, Rand explained the reason she chose architecture as the background and battlefield of this conflict:

> *I chose [architecture] because it is a field of work that covers both art and a basic need of men's survival. And because one cannot find a more eloquent symbol of man as creator than a man who is a builder. His antithesis, the collectivists, are destroyers.*[6]

Left *From Rand's notes about Howard Roark for* The Fountainhead, *February 9, 1936. Drafts for all of her novels and articles were written in longhand.*

Below: *Rand's "sharp, angular" practice signatures for her character Howard Roark*

The Fountainhead focuses specifically on the debate between proponents of classical and modern, "form-follows-function," architecture. But Rand's use of contemporary culture as a setting had grown more sophisticated than that employed in *We the Living*. Instead of referring directly to real people, such as Lenin and Trotsky, as she did in *We the Living*, the characters in *The Fountainhead* are literary abstractions derived from such contemporary figures as Gertrude Stein, William Randolph Hearst, and British socialist Harold Laski. Rand's ultimate goal as a writer of fiction was to completely fabricate a world, eschewing allusions to actual persons or events, and thus *The Fountainhead* was not her "ideal novel." Nevertheless, it was to be her first complete literary portrait of the "ideal man," a project she had been exploring and refining since her earliest attempts at writing fiction.

With credits including both a published novel and a successful Broadway play, Rand turned once again to Hollywood for work. Ann Watkins, her agent, had a track record of obtaining motion-picture writing assignments for New York writers. Rand had obtained these assignments for herself in the early 1930s, despite her relative obscurity in Hollywood, but having now earned a literary following, she expected more money and offers to work on more prominent films. Watkins, however, was unable to produce results working on her behalf, a failure a Hollywood associate of hers attributed to Rand's criticism of Soviet Russia. Rand later said that she was "literally blacklisted in those years."

Rand had corresponded regularly with her family since leaving Russia in 1926 and always harbored the hope that one day the family would be reunited in the United States. In 1936, she was heartbroken to receive a letter announcing that her sister Nora had fallen in love and was married, thereby making her emigration highly unlikely. Rand redoubled her efforts to secure permission for the emigration of her mother and father, but in May 1937 a telegram from them revealed that the Soviet government had denied their request to leave Russia. Shortly thereafter, the United States Post Office issued a public warning that an American writing a letter to a Soviet citizen could place the recipient in danger of reprisal from Soviet authorities. Rand stopped writing, despite the fact that her mother's letters continued to arrive, with increasingly alarmed pleas for Rand to write back. And then, without any explanation, all communication stopped.

The Fountainhead was a long-term project with an uncertain completion date. Unable to secure an advance on the unwritten novel, she relied once again on freelance reading of literary properties in English, French, German, and Russian for Hollywood studios, but this work drastically reduced the amount of time she was able to devote to *The Fountainhead*. However, she continued to outline the plot and began the required architectural research, studying books suggested by a librarian at the New York Public Library, and later working as a file clerk at the architectural firm of Ely Jacques Kahn.

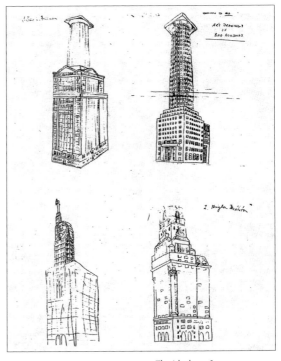

Eclectic architectural designs gathered as research for The Fountainhead. *Copied in her hand are works by (top to bottom, left to right) Matthew Freeman, Adolf Loos, Heinrich Mossdorf, and L. Bayer Pendelton.*

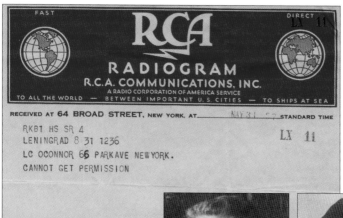

RKB1 HS SR 4
LENINGRAD 8 31 1236
LC OCONNOR 66 PARKAVE NEWYORK.
CANNOT GET PERMISSION

Telephone: HAnover 2-1811

Rand's father and mother, 1930s. After years of effort and false hopes, Rand received this telegram with the Soviet government's final decision regarding her parent's application for a visa to visit America. In the late 1940s Rand learned that her father had died in 1939 and her mother in 1940, both of natural causes. Her sister Natalia died during a World War II air raid, while Nora's status remained unknown.

In 1936 theatrical producer Jerome Mayer read *We the Living* and approached Rand with the suggestion that her book would make an effective stage play, which Rand hoped would promote book sales. Mayer optioned the play and Rand began working on the stage adaptation.

In the summer of 1937 Frank O'Connor, still working as an actor, was cast in a summer stock version of *Night of January 16th* in Stony Creek, Connecticut. Later, Rand joined her husband, taking a break from *The Fountainhead* in order to write a new work entitled *Anthem*. Her shortest novel, originally conceived as a play, *Anthem* projects, in ornate, poetic prose, a futuristic society in which the word "I" has been dropped from the vocabularies (and minds) of human beings. The story concerns a young street sweeper who rediscovers electricity but is denounced by a society unwilling to advance beyond tallow candles. Persecuted for his independence, he escapes into the "Uncharted Forest," where he rediscovers the word "I" and the "meaning of man's ego." Ann Watkins was unable to draw interest from publishers in the United States (where it remained unpublished until 1946), but Cassell and Company published the book in Britain, where it was a critical success.

Even while she was working on *Anthem,* Rand continued to think about and work on *The Fountainhead.* After she completed one-third of the novel, her agent submitted the first chapters to publishers, which resulted in a long series of rejection letters. Her job as a studio reader continued to pay bills, and O'Connor found

From Frank O'Connor's "actor's composite," ca. 1930s. "All my heroes will always be reflections of Frank."[7]

Rand and her friend Albert Mannheimer, Stony Creek, Connecticut, summer 1937. Mannheimer, who later wrote numerous screenplays, including Born Yesterday *(1950), had been an avowed communist and, along with writer Budd Schulberg, visited Moscow in the early 1930s. Rand converted Mannheimer to capitalism in "a little under a year."*

work as a cigar store clerk. In 1939 Rand wrote a philosophical mystery drama called "Think Twice," in which she attempted to expose "the evil of altruism, and the need of man to live an independent, egoistic existence."[7] It was an enjoyable writing project that took only a few weeks to complete, but despite some initial encouragement, it did not raise serious interest from producers. Meanwhile, Jerome Mayer had been unable to sell investors on his idea for a theatrical production of *We the Living*. However, in August 1939 renowned Broadway producer George Abbott acquired the theatrical rights, and in February 1940 he presented the play, retitled *The Unconquered,* at the Biltmore Theatre. The critical response—even from those sympathetic to Rand's ideas—was uniformly negative, and the play closed after six performances.

The election of 1940 was another event that drew Rand's attention and energy away from writing *The Fountainhead*. Eight years into the administration of FDR, whose New Deal policies Rand viewed as antithetical to capitalism and individualism, a strong counter-movement of young conservatives had begun to form, and in New York City, a right-wing intellectual circle parallel to the Algonquin Round Table had gathered. Rand and O'Connor, subsisting on the last of their savings, volunteered full-time at the Wendell Willkie campaign's headquarters in Manhattan. Within several weeks, Rand had organized an "intellectual ammunition bureau," which aimed to expose the failures of New Deal policies. This was also the occasion of her first major public speaking engagements, which included question-and-answer periods following pro-Willkie newsreels at a Union Square movie theater. Despite her passionate work on Willkie's behalf, Rand ultimately grew disillusioned with what she considered an unprincipled campaign. In the November elections, Roosevelt triumphed over Willkie in a landslide, gaining 449 electoral votes to Willkie's 82. Rand's bitterness during this time is illustrated by one of her

Al Hirschfeld's drawing of the cast of The Unconquered *in the* New York Times, *February 11, 1940. Left to right: Georgina Brand, Arthur Pierson, Edwin Philips, Lea Penman, John Emery, Helen Craig, and Dean Jagger.*

letters from this period. She was invited by novelist Dashiell Hammett to attend a benefit to oppose Social Justice, the domestic Fascist group led by Father Charles Coughlin. The event was hosted by Lillian Hellman, Hammett's lover and a prominent voice of the Left. Rand wrote back to Hammett that she would welcome an invitation to fight Coughlin when Hammett gave a party "to fight *both* 'Social Justice' and *The Daily Worker*," ending her letter, "Not until then, Comrade, not until then."[8]

Following the election, and after *The Fountainhead* had been rejected by eleven publishers, Rand severed her professional relationship with Ann Watkins. She returned to studio reading, and a sympathetic story editor at Paramount Pictures, Richard Mealand, offered to contact a publisher on her behalf. Rand suggested Little, Brown and submitted the book herself. As she remembers, within a month, editor Angus Cameron met with her and related the editorial board's report, which included the following comment: "This is a work of almost genius, genius in the power of its expression, almost in the sense of its enormous bitterness." Cameron, Rand later recalled, extolled the work as "high-grade literature, very intellectual," and lamented that there was no readership for it. The rejection was the twelfth, and the most disappointing yet. She decided to stop working on the book. Recounting Little, Brown's reaction to the manuscript, she recalled what she said to Frank, "If someone doesn't appreciate it, well that's their bad standards. But to have it rejected because it's too good, that was really a feeling of horror." In response, Frank rallied her spirits during the course of a despairing night, arguing that one should not give up the world to those whom one despises. By the next morning, she had regained her resolve and returned to work. Later, she broke her own rule against book dedications by dedicating the book to her husband, who had saved it.

Rand contacted Mealand with the suggestion to try Bobbs-Merrill, which had just released Eugene Lyons's *The Red Decade: The Stalinist Penetration of America*, a journalistic account of the negative influence of the Communist Party on American culture. Archibald Ogden, a young, recently hired editor, who by first

appearance and temperament seemed to Rand to be the exact
opposite of the ideals embodied in the manuscript on his desk,
met with Rand and agreed to consider the book for Bobbs-Merrill,
the thirteenth publisher to see it.

```
Rejected by:

        Knopf
        Simon & Schuster
        Reynal & Hitchcock
        Lippincott
        Dodd Mead
        Doubleday Doran
        Harcourt Brace
        Macmillan
        Duell, Sloan & Pearce
        Stokes
        Dutton
        Random House (Outline Submitted)
```

Above *Rand's list of publishers
who rejected* The Fountainhead

Right *Archibald Ogden, Rand's
editor at Bobbs-Merrill*

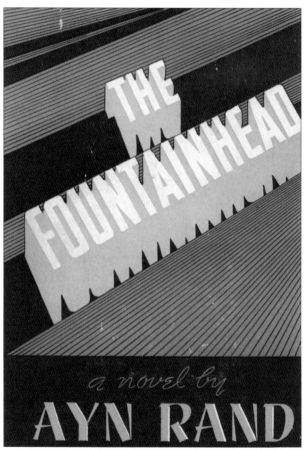

Dust jacket for The Fountainhead, *1943*

The Real
1943–1950

The telegram read: "If this is not the book for you, then I
am not the editor for you." The sender was Archibald
Ogden and the recipient the editor-in-chief of Bobbs-
Merrill. Ogden had read and responded to *The
Fountainhead* manuscript within a week, praising the novel
in the highest possible terms. Once again, an editorial
board had a mixed opinion, but Ogden's enthusiasm was
the deciding factor. Rand signed a contract on December
10, 1941, to complete and deliver the manuscript by the
end of 1942. Because the advance was insufficient to cover
her living expenses, Richard Mealand arranged for her to
continue working as a reader for Paramount Pictures.

In the year following the Willkie campaign and leading
up to meeting Ogden, Rand had expanded her network of
New York conservative intellectuals. While writing *The
Fountainhead* in 1941, she approached Channing Pollock, a
drama critic and playwright, to help her start a "an intellectual union of conservatives," which they called The
Individualist Organization. Rand's goal was to fill the vacu-
um left by the Willkie defeat. In a letter to Pollock she wrote:

> Our side has no "ideology," no clear-cut, consistent system of
> belief, no philosophy of life. . . . The first aim of our organiza-
> tion will be intellectual and philosophical—not merely politi-
> cal and economic.[1]

Turns With a Bookworm

Oh, we might as well answer a perennial question about Ayn Rand—yes, she looks exactly like her photographs; smooth black hair, round eyes that look black and aren't, neat figure and just that turn of the head and direct gaze and natural simplicity of manner. . . . She likes cats, architecture, New York, movies and above all, ideas. . . . She is afraid of traffic because she was hit by a taxi once; and the way she shows it is to stand a minute at the crossing, viewing the stream of vehicles with alarm, seize the hand of her escort with a gesture of feminine terror, and then march ahead across the street, hauling her protector after her.

Isabel Paterson, ca. 1943. Her "Turns With a Bookworm" column, New York Herald Tribune, September 23, 1945, features a short profile of Rand.

During this period her most significant friendship—one that grew into an intense intellectual exchange—was with the brilliant and fiery Isabel Paterson, book columnist for the *New York Herald Tribune* and author of *The God of the Machine*. Rand began a spirited correspondence with "Pat," delighted to find someone whose interest in philosophy and history matched her own. Their relationship continued until the late 1940s, when it ended over personal and philosophical differences.

With Rand's political activism and feverish effort to finish *The Fountainhead*, she became a "writing engine," a phrase she coined for herself in her early twenties. During one session, she wrote continuously for thirty hours, in longhand, and in the weeks before her deadline she raced to type up the handwritten pages. She delivered her manuscript to the Bobbs-Merrill office on December 31, 1942, inscribing on it: "10:38 a.m."

The Fountainhead was published on May 8, 1943. Rand estimated that she would have to sell 100,000 copies in order to reach her kind of reader. Paterson, while sympathetic, was nevertheless shocked to hear this number. As a published novelist and book reviewer, Pat knew how rare it was for a book to sell in that quantity. In order to have any chance to reach that many readers, a concerted effort would be required in the areas of marketing and publicity, the responsibility of which rested entirely with Bobbs-Merrill. However, Rand was displeased by the first advertisements, which glossed over the book's philosophical content and highlighted the love story of the main characters, Howard Roark and Dominique Francon.

No less displeasing to Rand were the initial reviews, which also tended to elide Rand's principal theme—the conflict between individualism and collectivism—and suggest that the novel was mostly about architecture. This led to a feeling of frustration and resignation on Rand's part: if *The Fountainhead* did not establish her fame, she believed that she could expect no recognition at all during her lifetime. However, on May 16th, the *New York Times* published Lorine Pruette's review of the book and Ogden sent Rand an advance copy.

Ayn Rand, wrote Pruette, "has written a hymn in praise of the individual . . . you will not be able to read this masterful book without thinking through some of the basic concepts of our times." Two days later, in a letter to Pruette, Rand responded: "You have said that I am a writer of great power. Yet I feel completely helpless to express my gratitude to you for your review of my novel." Rand praised Pruette's courage for writing the review in a climate in which, she feared, "one was no longer permitted to speak in defense of the Individual" and in which discussing individualism in a review might be "too dangerous." Pruette, wrote Rand, had saved her from the horror of believing that "this country is lost, that people are much more rotten than I presented

Percy Crosby's "Skippy," distributed by King Features Syndicate, Inc. in 1943, and kept by Rand in a file called "Misc. clippings (Political & Cultural) (from the California period)"

Posters for the release of Noi Vivi and Addio, Kira!, the 1942 Italian two-part, pirated film adaptation of We the Living. Until it was banned, the film played in Axis and Axis-occupied countries. Re-released in 1986 as We the Living, the film was partly re-edited by Rand.

them in the book, and that there is no intellectual decency left anywhere."[2] Eighteen years later, Rand said that Pruette's review "saved my universe in that period. . . . I expected nothing like that from the *Times*. And it's the only intelligent review I have really had in my whole career as far as novels are concerned."

The Fountainhead and its author had been successfully launched. However, another concern of that time, Rand's effort to form an "individualist organization," failed. In a letter to Channing Pollock, she remarked that the left was winning, not merely because of their economic arguments for Communism, but because

> [t]hey provide, first, an intellectual justification—a faith in collective action, in unlimited majority power, in a general, leveling equality, in "unselfishness," "service," etc. What are the intellectual justifications for our side? What are our moral values? Who has defined it? Who is preaching philosophical individualism? No one. And if it is not preached, economic individualism will not survive.[3]

Having failed to reach conservative intellectuals, Rand redirected her appeal to the business sector. She thought that a novel defending the morality of individualism would appeal to their self-interest, so she began soliciting money for advertisements that would raise awareness of *The Fountainhead* and its ideas. She argued that business leaders needed a moral sanction, that it was not merely practical but also moral to be productive and seek personal profit. But she discovered that businessmen, as a rule, disparaged philosophy as impractical.

However, the practical importance of ideas was receiving a powerful demonstration in World War II, in which ideological conflicts were being settled on battlefields. During the war, Mussolini's Fascist government pirated *We the Living* and approved a film adaptation in two parts, entitled *Noi Vivi* and *Addio Kira*. The film was directed by Goffredo Alessandrini and starred Alida Valli and Rossano Brazzi, and was released in Italy in 1942. The film was purported to be an indictment of the Soviet Union, Italy's wartime enemy, but after enormous success at the box office, Italian and German censors began to realize what made the film so appealing to audiences—that its themes could be construed just as easily as an attack on Fascism—and they banned further screenings. All prints of the film were ordered to be destroyed.

Despite wartime anxiety and hardship, *The Fountainhead* was finding its audience in the United States, and by November 1943 the book had sold more than 18,000 copies. Rand received considerable fan mail, to which she replied, often at lengths of more than ten single-spaced typewritten pages, answering philosophical and literary questions posed by her readers, with topics ranging from an examination of Howard Roark's character and the mythology of Jesus to political and literary advice.

One topic in these fan letters was the relationship between the character Howard Roark and the architect Frank Lloyd Wright. In a 1951 letter to a college student, she wrote:

> *You may be justified in seeing some parallel between Howard Roark and Frank Lloyd Wright only in a strictly architectural sense, that is, in the fact that both are great fighters for modern architecture. . . . [T]here is no resemblance whatever between Roark's personal character and the character of Mr. Wright, between the events of their lives, and between their fundamental philosophies of life.*[4]

Frank Godwin's drawing of Howard Roark for King Features's "Illustrated Fountainhead." This serialized condensation of 30 episodes was written by Rand and appeared in 36 newspapers beginning in December 1945.

Facing page *This portrait by Talbot for* The Fountainhead *dust jacket remained Rand's favorite photograph of herself.*

In 1937 Wright had rebuffed Rand's request to meet and interview him. Eventually, he read and praised the novel ("your thesis is *the* great one," he wrote[5]) and later invited Rand and O'Connor to his Wisconsin estate, Taliesin, which she praised as "magnificent." But the visit wasn't a pleasant one. She found Wright's students to be awestruck hero-worshippers, and she had philosophical differences with Wright's wife. However, despite the fact that there was no meeting of the minds between Rand and Wright, she greatly admired his architectural accomplishments, writing to him in 1944, "I felt, whenever I entered a building of yours [that] here one had to be a hero and lead a heroic life."[6]

Rand secured a new agent, Alan Collins, to handle the sale of the motion picture rights to *The Fountainhead*. Though the book continued to sell, sales still fell far short of the 100,000-copy objective, and having worked in Hollywood, Rand was well aware of how a successful screen adaptation could boost a book's sales. Collins recommended an asking price of $25,000 for the rights, which Rand rejected as too low. She suggested $50,000, which Collins reluctantly presented to Warner Bros. Studios after the company expressed interest. In October 1943, following another frustrating luncheon with a businessman who declined her request for advertising funds, Rand returned to her New York apartment and found her husband standing in the living room with an "abnormal" look on his face: "Well, darling," he announced, "you've earned $50,000 while you were out to lunch." Collins had left word that Warner Bros. had acceded to her demands. In late 1943 Rand and O'Connor returned to Hollywood, where she would begin her second phase as a screenwriter.

Henry Blanke, a Warner Bros. producer with a long résumé of critically acclaimed, successful films, had read *The Fountainhead* and, with the help of actress Barbara Stanwyck, persuaded the studio to purchase the property. The deal called for Rand to write the preliminary script, which Blanke thought should remain as faithful to the book as possible. The first draft took six weeks to complete and was 283 pages long, twice the length of the final version. Pleased with her work, Blanke offered Rand a full-time writing contract. However, she

The O'Connors' Chatsworth "ranch" (the von Sternberg House), designed in 1935 by Richard Neutra for director Josef von Sternberg and demolished in 1971

Rand on the grounds of Chatsworth "ranch," ca. 1940s

was already planning her next novel and countered Blanke's offer, suggesting a work calendar of six months on and six months off. The studio refused, but Hal Wallis, who had recently signed a producing deal with Paramount Pictures, agreed to her terms.

Due to rationing of materials during World War II, production on the film was delayed. When it became apparent that he and Rand would not return immediately to New York, O'Connor began looking for a residential/investment property. After considering Frank Lloyd Wright's Storer House, located six blocks from the small West Hollywood apartment in which Rand had worked on *We the Living* in 1933, he selected a house by Richard Neutra. Originally built for director Josef von Sternberg, the steel-and-glass house was located on a thirteen-acre property in the Chatsworth area of the San Fernando Valley. Thoroughly disenchanted with film and stage acting, O'Connor spent the following years developing the ranch into a commercial enterprise, growing alfalfa and cut flowers.

Rand settled into California life but remained a New Yorker at heart. In a 1943 letter to Archibald Ogden, she compared the two cities:

> I hate Hollywood as a place, just as I did before. It's overcrowded, vulgar, cheap and sad in a hopeless sort of way. The people on the streets are all tense, eager, suspicious and look unhappy. The has-beens and the would-bes. I don't think anything in the world is worth this kind of struggle.
>
> I miss New York, in a strange way, with a homesickness I've never felt before for any place on earth. I'm in love with New York, and I don't mean I love it, but I mean I'm in love with it. Frank says that what I love is not the real city, but the New York I built myself. That's true.[7]

Although the demands of her career kept her in Hollywood, the years 1943 through 1951 yielded opportunities and challenges in several aspects: financial, political, intellectual, and social.

Right *Rand and O'Connor with Gary Cooper on the set of* The Fountainhead, ca. 1948.

Left *One of the many posters created by Warner Bros. for its 1949 release of* The Fountainhead.

Below *An ad placed by Bobbs-Merrill in conjunction with the 1949 release of the film version of* The Fountainhead.

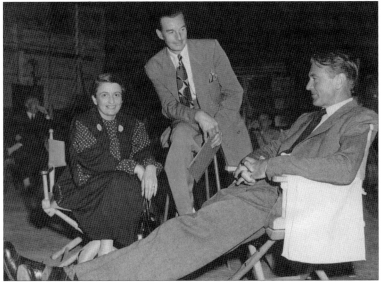

Financially, her Paramount contract provided regular and significant income. She adapted numerous properties for Wallis, two of which were produced: *Love Letters*, directed by William Dieterle and starring Jennifer Jones and Joseph Cotten, and, with writer Robert Smith, *You Came Along*, directed by John Farrow and starring Robert Cummings and Lizabeth Scott.

The Fountainhead had become a major success, selling 150,000 copies by July 1945, and becoming a fixture on bestseller lists. While the film, directed by King Vidor and starring Gary Cooper and Patricia Neal, became the promotional vehicle she had hoped for—upon its release in July 1949, the novel returned to the bestseller lists—the production was a torturous experience. With the exception of her script and her initial enthusiasm for the casting of Cooper, she "disliked the movie from beginning to end." She found the acting "embarrassing," the pacing "too fast," the art direction plain "bad," and Vidor's direction "unimaginative" and "naturalistic." After a contentious battle over control of

Rand testifying before the House Un-American Activities Committee, October 20, 1947. When asked in 1976 to comment on Lillian Hellman's Hollywood blacklist memoir, Scoundrel Time, she replied, in part: "I'll say only this. All those filthy god damned Communists are boasting about their courage, such as Lillian Hellman, who was a member of the Communist Party. How many people died in this country, and in Russia, or in Russia-occupied countries because of Miss Hellman's ideas, god only knows. Nobody could compute the evil of what those Communists in the 1930s did."

the shooting script, Rand's version was shot as written; however, on the night of the Hollywood premiere, she discovered that the studio had deleted a line from Roark's final courtroom speech: "I came here to say that I am a man who does not exist for others." This was enough to numb any joy or sense of triumph Rand experienced at the premiere.

Rand remained politically active during this period in Hollywood, where she was voted onto the board of the Motion Picture Alliance for the Preservation of American Ideals, an organization of conservatives and liberals that exposed the subtle use of totalitarian propaganda in films. Her major contribution was "Screen Guide for Americans," a pamphlet in which she explained common propaganda techniques. This guide established her credentials as an expert on Communist propaganda, and attracted the notice of the House Un-American Activities Committee, before which she was subpoenaed to testify in 1947 in Washington, D.C. Despite doubts about the efficacy of the committee, she approved of its stated goal—to investigate attempts by a foreign power to violently overthrow the U.S. government—and was confident that freedom of speech was not being abrogated. She remarked that "Congress has no right to inquire into ideas or opinions, but has every right to inquire into criminal activities. Belonging to [the Communist Party, an] organization that advocates criminal actions, comes into the sphere of the criminal, not the ideological."[8] She prepared comments on two films, but was not called to comment on *The Best Years of Our Lives,* a popular film in current release; instead, she was forced to confine her testimony to *Song of Russia*, an inept and obviously pro-Soviet film released four years earlier. Rand left Washington in a state of frustration, sure that the plan to expose Communist propaganda would wither under the committee's ineptitude.

Meanwhile, her ideas continued to flourish and develop. The first six-month break from screenwriting was productive. She read philosophy systematically and, following a suggestion by an editor at Bobbs-Merrill, began writing "The Moral Basis of Individualism," a nonfiction presentation of the philosophical ideas in *The Fountainhead*. After several drafts of this work, she discovered that a truly successful book of this type would require her to further develop certain ideas in metaphysics (which concerns the nature of reality) and epistemology (the theory of knowledge) that underlay the ethical and political theories that were the book's primary concern.

Rand and O'Connor with their "close acquaintance" and neighbor, costume designer Adrian (left), who was married to actress Janet Gaynor, and an unidentified woman (right).

Leonebel Jacobs's companion portrait of Rand, 1948

"The best of my material possessions," Rand said of this 1948 pastel portrait of O'Connor by Leonebel Jacobs.[9]

Leonebel Jacobs drawing O'Connor in the living room of the Chatsworth house, 1948

And since merely restating the ideas of *The Fountainhead* did not interest her, she stopped work on the project.

Socially, the thirteen-acre Chatsworth ranch was a striking back-drop for frequent weekend visits from new Hollywood acquaintances and old New York friends. Visitors included fans, fellow writers, publishers, actors, designers, Hollywood political activists, and, on one occasion, a political science class from a local college.

Rand was about five feet four inches tall and often wore ready-to-wear designs or casual outfits quickly thrown together. Her short, brown hair softly framed her face, the most prominent feature of which was her dark, penetrating eyes. Businesslike at work, she was normally polite and gracious, but as soon as a conversation turned to philosophical subjects, her eyes would light up. She answered questions directly, her Russian-accented voice probing every implication exhaustively. Philosophy was not, she held, an intellectual game, but a practical, life-and-death matter. This view shaped her character and temperament in many respects. When she felt other people showed signs of being influenced by what she considered to be wrong and dangerous ideas, her contempt for those ideas became anger at times. Her long-time friend Leonard Peikoff commented:

> I asked her once—when I was much younger—why she got so emo-tionally upset at the theories of philosophers like Immanuel Kant. And she said to me, "Because when I hear a philosopher say there is no reality and your mind is totally invalid, that means all your values are nullified: your husband, your love, your work, the music you like, your freedom". . . Most people hear abstractions as, simply, floating abstractions. But, for her, she translated it into the actual concrete things that it meant and what it would mean in her own life. And she was able to react emotionally to broad abstractions, which very few people can do.[10]

The values Rand affirmed were manifold: her Adrian-designed clothing, blue-green jewelry, agates, cats, her favorite phonograph records filling the atrium of the Neutra-designed home with record-ed music that she followed with her own baton—and, most of all, her work and her husband. She attended to these things with pas-

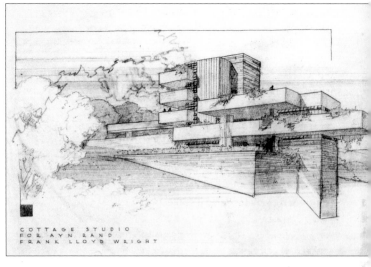

COTTAGE STUDIO
FOR AYN RAND
FRANK LLOYD WRIGHT

"The house you designed for me was magnificent," Rand wrote to Frank Lloyd Wright. "I gasped when I saw it. It is the particular kind of sculpture in space which I love and which nobody but you has ever been able to achieve. Most personally: Thank you for the fountain. That was as if you had autographed both my house and my book."[11] Designed by Wright in 1946 but never built.

sion, and she expected the same of others as they pursued *their* own values. The extremes of joy and anger she felt were a consequence of her deep-seated belief that moral judgment is essential to the preservation and enjoyment of human life. "When one pronounces moral judgment, whether in praise or in blame, one must be prepared to answer 'Why?'"[12] At times, Rand's own judgment of people, though she always sought to base it on fact, was in error, and her disapproval (or approval) of them was mistaken. However, her moral absolutism was grounded in her belief in the life-sustaining power of philosophy, and anger and condemnation were never her defining qualities. In defense of her ideas, she pulled no punches with dilettantes or disingenuous intellectuals. She also spared no effort in praising or reaching out to those who took ideas seriously.

Frank with Oscar and Oswald, ca. 1943. "[Oscar and Oswald] are two lion cubs (stuffed), and they are supposed to represent the bad sides of Frank's character. Whenever he pulls a bad joke, he blames it on Oswald; and whenever he loses his temper, it's supposed to be Oscar growling. That's how it all started, but now they have become very much members of our household."[13]

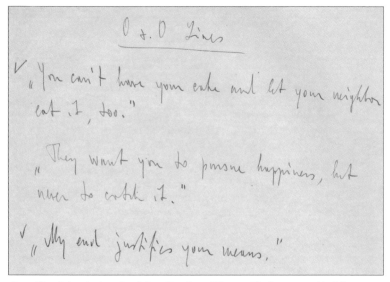

O & O Lines

✓ "You can't have your cake and let your neighbor eat it, too."

"They want you to pursue happiness, but never to catch it."

✓ "My end justifies your means."

Part of Rand's handwritten list of clever lines from O'Connor. The first was used in Atlas Shrugged *(p. 464), and the second appeared in a letter to Isabel Paterson.*[14] *"O. & O. Lines" is a play on words on the names Oscar and Oswald, the stuffed lion cubs.*

The Strike
1951–1957

In 1951 Rand and O'Connor returned to New York City, the setting for her next novel, *Atlas Shrugged*. Rand described the theme of *Atlas Shrugged* as "the role of the mind in man's existence—and, as a corollary, the demonstration of a new moral philosophy: the morality of rational self-interest."[1] The idea for the novel occurred to her in 1943, while discussing the philosophy of *The Fountainhead* with an acquaintance who insisted that Rand was obligated to enlighten her readers with a nonfiction version of her ethical philosophy. Rand countered she had already fulfilled the obligation and that her case was clear to any attentive reader of her fiction. However, she wondered aloud, "What would happen if every creative person went on strike against such obligations?" That, she exclaimed, would make a good novel. After the discussion ended, O'Connor, who was in the room at the time, turned to her and said: "It *would* make a good novel."[2]

Rand thought that "The Mind on Strike" would be a relatively short work dealing with economics, and that it would "illustrate [*The Fountainhead*'s] philosophy in action [and] merely show that capitalism and the proper economics rest on the mind." But as she further examined the mind's role in human existence, the scope of the novel expanded. Eventually, the finished novel integrated a wide range of topics, including metaphysics, politics, and romantic love. She thought the novel would require two years to write; instead, it would take fourteen years. *The Fountainhead*, as she later put it, was merely an overture to *Atlas Shrugged*.

Left *Rand and O'Connor at the 1950 wedding of her secretary, June Kato, to George Kurisu. Working on the weekends while she attended college, June was the first typist for* Atlas Shrugged. *The Katos all worked at the ranch after their release from a Japanese-American internment camp. Rand regarded the internment of American citizens during World War II as an injustice arising from collectivist New Deal policies.*

Ashtray depicting a steel mill in Atlas Shrugged—*designed by Sasha Brastoff for Rand and O'Connor*

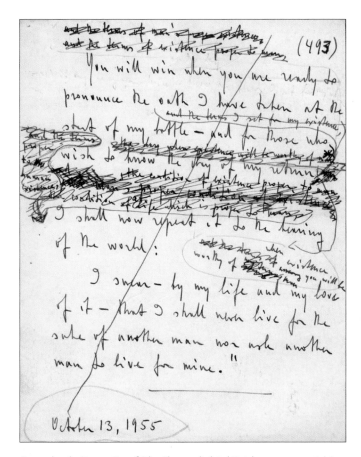

From a handwritten section of Atlas Shrugged, *dated October 13, 1955, containing the oath of the men of the mind on strike.*

Originally titled "The Strike," the book was renamed *Atlas Shrugged,* formerly the name of a chapter. With its allusion to Greek mythology, the revised title expressed a characteristic that made the book her "ideal novel": its conflicts and events were "completely detached from any journalistic reality." With a plot featuring a strike that united industrialists, artists, and laborers,

Atlas Shrugged was set in a world conceived entirely of her own imagination.

The story of *Atlas Shrugged* concerns men and women of ability in all fields, who are oppressed by a collectivist world that refuses to recognize their value. The background is modern industrial civilization. When the story opens, New York City is crumbling. Every manner of sacrifice of the individual to "the greater good" has been practiced in accordance with every known religious or philosophical viewpoint, yet living conditions are getting worse. The world's generator is running down, but no one knows why. Against this backdrop, Rand would present and dramatize her entire philosophy.

The scope of the story required that she formulate her own views on numerous philosophical issues, including the origin of values, the nature of volition, the law of identity as the bridge between metaphysics and epistemology, the finitude of space and time, and the nature of universals. When a philosophical issue arose during

At Harmon, Indiana, aboard the Twentieth Century Limited during the "research" ride she later described as "the greatest experience in my life," November 23, 1947.

Rand at work on Atlas Shrugged, *July 1949*

the writing of the novel, she would think about it for several days and then, in one or two attempts, resolve the problem it posed before resuming her writing. Although she found no difficulty in this process, she did struggle to integrate the philosophical themes into a compelling plot. Placing philosophical speeches within a story of a secret strike was a grueling task that required seamless juxtaposition of theoretical abstractions and literary constructs. "Fiction," she observed, "required breaking up of philosophic abstractions into concrete reality . . . [and] this always had the feeling of impeding what I wanted to say." The final manuscript was the product of laborious revision. Rand rewrote every page, on average, five times.

Rand began submitting the book to publishers when she finished the major philosophical speech, a nearly 35,000-word summary of her entire philosophy that took two years to complete. Her primary concern was how a publisher would handle a radical and controver-

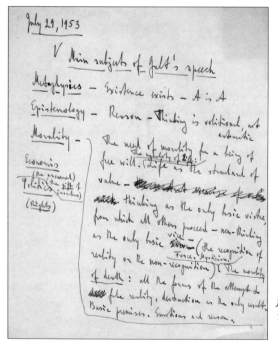

Facing page *Dollar-sign cigarettes were one of the promotional gimmicks used by Random House to publicize* Atlas Shrugged

"Main subjects of Galt's speech" from Rand's notes for Atlas Shrugged *dated July 29, 1953*

sial book certain to antagonize the critics. After meeting with several publishers, Rand found Random House to be the most receptive to her concerns. President Bennett Cerf, assuring her that Random House was no longer the left-wing bastion of the 1930s and 40s, proposed that she submit the book to several houses simultaneously and compare their marketing approaches. Donald Klopfer, Cerf's partner, perceptively grasped the book's theme, suggesting that a moral defense of capitalism would clash with the entire Judeo-Christian ethical tradition. The understanding of Cerf and Klopfer earned Rand's enthusiasm, and she signed a contract with Random House, which published *Atlas Shrugged* on October 10, 1957.

As expected, the book was attacked by critics. Granville Hicks, the former Macmillan editor who had opposed the publication of *We the Living*, wrote a disparaging review in the *New York Times*. Whittaker Chambers, famous for his role in the Alger Hiss espionage case, wrote a similarly vitriolic review for *The National Review*. Opposition came from across the American spectrum. Catholics and religious conservatives hated its atheism and egoism. Liberals were offended by its glorification of laissez-faire capitalism. The middle-of-the-road was bewildered by its uncompromising tone. Almost universally, the critics rejected the book's philosophy and dismissed the writing as blatant propaganda.

One of many photos taken of Rand by Bennett Cerf's wife, Phyllis, for the dust jacket of Atlas Shrugged. *When Rand worked in the RKO wardrobe department, she had provided costumes to Phyllis Fraser (later Cerf), a teenage actress at RKO.*

The reaction stunned Random House, but what shocked Rand was "the abysmal, stupid, hooliganism of the reviews. That they were self-contradictory even within their own terms. Total distortions, and that there was nobody objecting to it. That the whole state of the culture suddenly appeared much worse than I had imagined." At first, sales were stunted by the poor reviews, but, carried along by word-of-mouth, within two months of its publication, *Atlas Shrugged* ranked in the top ten of the *New York Times* bestseller list. It remained there for eighteen weeks.

Writing the novel had used every literary "circuit" she possessed, and completing it fulfilled a life-long goal: she had presented the ideal man and the philosophy that made him

Rand and O'Connor in their apartment at 36 E. 36th St. (known as "the perfect 36"), where she completed Atlas Shrugged *on March 20, 1957*

possible, successfully projecting this ideal in the characters of dozens of men and women. However, the critical reception to the novel was a rude awakening to the vast distance that separated her views from the mainstream.

In the early 1950s, while writing the novel, Rand began to meet informally with a group of fans, first in California and later in New York, to discuss her views and, later, to read the novel-in-progress. They were young people attracted to the ideas expressed in *The Fountainhead*, and the members of this circle, whom she wryly referred to as the "the Collective," became her main social contacts. Its nine original members included: Nathan Blumenthal (later Nathaniel Branden), a psychologist; Leonard Peikoff, a future philosopher and Rand's intellectual and legal heir; and Alan Greenspan, the future chairman of the Federal Reserve Board. Throughout the 1950s she enjoyed the weekly gatherings at her apartment as a welcome break from her writing. These discussions were an extension of the world of her novel. However, the issues raised by the "Collective," drawn from their university studies and careers and reflective of the real state of the world, often raised to Rand the disturbing thought that the intellectual climate of the real world was far worse than that depicted in her novel.

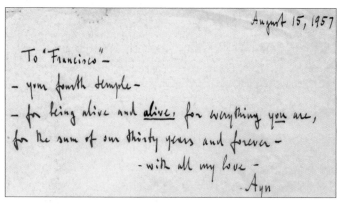

Rand's practice dedication to her husband for his copy of Atlas Shrugged

With the 1957 publication of *Atlas Shrugged*, her *magnum opus* was finished. Rand was fifty-two years old, at the peak of her powers, and facing a troubling thought: she might never find another "big assignment" in a world she considered to be intellectually bankrupt.

Above *Rand with Nathaniel Branden, 1955*

Right *From left to right: Rand, O'Connor, Barbara Branden, Leonard Peikoff, Alan Greenspan, and Joan Blumenthal, members of the "Collective," who read* Atlas Shrugged *in manuscript form, ca. 1950s.*

14K, 7/8-inch-long miniature gold bar, a present to Rand from Alan Greenspan to commemorate the publication of Atlas Shrugged. *Engraved on top:* MULLIGAN BANK. *Engraved on bottom:* ACCOUNT OF AYN RAND, OCT. 10, 1957.

A Philosophy for Living on Earth 1958–1968

Rand was facing a crisis of identity in the post–*Atlas Shrugged* period. The "worst part," she said, was "that I could not make up my mind am I a fiction writer or a philosopher." Neither could she determine the audience for her ideas. She experienced two extreme and conflicting states: the publication of the novel gave her a profound sense of fulfillment, but the resistance to her ideas expressed in numerous reviews and articles, most painfully from members of her own generation, was a source of nearly unbearable pain and frustration.

In the past, she had been drawn to fiction as a means of concretizing her concept of "the ideal man," and having completed *Atlas Shrugged,* she had nothing further to express in this regard. "Ivory tower" philosophizing did not interest her. It never had. She assumed that a competent academic of the day would step forward to present her views in an appropriate form, but a series of conversations with Branden and Peikoff convinced her that the philosophy in *Atlas Shrugged* was an epochal break with past philosophy and that no such academic existed.

According to Rand, twentieth-century professors and writers, from Analytic philosophers to Pragmatists to Existentialists to Zen Buddhists, had a common message: man's mind is incapable of attaining reliable knowledge of the world. In the post-*Atlas Shrugged* period, she concluded that the culture at large was waiting for a reality-based philosophy that could actually guide one's life.

Daniel Greene, Portrait of Ayn Rand, ca. 1959. To get herself into the proper frame of mind during this sitting, Rand brought along a favorite recording of Emmerich Kálmán's operetta Die Csárdásfürstin.

The positive response to *Atlas Shrugged* from young people demonstrated that they were still seeking philosophical answers and still open to a radically new, systematic philosophy. However, she found the as-yet-unfulfilled promise of the younger generation insufficiently motivating. In the past, writing for "her kind of mind"— a totally independent and rational reader—was an important motivation, and she hoped that, with the availability of the fictional expression of her views in *Atlas Shrugged*, a defender would emerge, one who would be, in the words of Kay Gonda, the heroine of her play "Ideal," "an answering voice, an answering hymn, an echo."[1] "The Collective" provided her with a forum in which to discuss her ideas, but the fact that her views were unique and generally anathema to the philosophical community ultimately meant that she would never be able to find an intellectual peer (although, in her husband she did find a life-long spiritual equal). But Rand was personally motivated by the thought that "the ideal man does exist," in the fictional world she created if nowhere else, and she resolved to defend that ideal through the writing of nonfiction. Writing philosophy, she now concluded, would not be "too abstract," because she would be creating it "for Galt and for the characters in *Atlas Shrugged*."

Even so, Rand directed her effort toward actual human beings and their need of "a philosophy for living on earth":

> In order to live, man must act; in order to act, he must make choices; in order to make choices, he must define a code of values; in order to define a code of values, he must know what he is and where he is— i.e., he must know his own nature (including his means of knowledge) and the nature of the universe in which he acts—i.e., he needs metaphysics, epistemology, ethics, which means: philosophy.[2]

Her goal was to re-establish the importance of reason in Western culture and validate its efficacy. And this "big assignment," the culmination of a thought she had first had in her youth, revitalized her in the wake of the disappointing response to *Atlas Shrugged*.

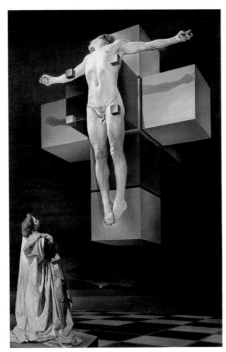

Salvador Dali, Corpus Hypercubus, *oil on canvas, 29" by 23," 1954. Rand's favorite painting—she spent hours contemplating it at the Metropolitan Museum of Art. She felt a kinship between her personal view of John Galt's defiance over his torture in* Atlas Shrugged *and Dali's depiction of the suffering of Jesus.*

She later recalled, "I was convinced at that time, and this goes as far back as I can remember—that's even before I knew the words 'metaphysics' and 'epistemology'—that the most important thing really is epistemology. And that the most important thing is the validity of your form of knowledge."

Reason was the core of the new systematic philosophy that she called "Objectivism," its name derived from her theory of objectivity:

Objectivity is both a metaphysical and epistemological concept. It pertains to the relationship of consciousness to existence. Metaphysically, it is the recognition of the fact that reality exists independent of any perceiver's consciousness. Epistemologically, it is the recognition of the fact that a perceiver's (man's) consciousness must acquire knowledge of reality by certain means (reason) in accordance with certain rules (logic).[3]

Objectivism, as she explained it in her first *Los Angeles Times* column in 1962, advocated reality, reason, self-interest, and capitalism. "Reality," she wrote, "exists as an objective absolute—facts are facts, independent of man's feelings, wishes, hopes or fears."[4] Reason is man's only source of knowledge and guide to action, and his basic means of survival. Survival requires an ethics of rational self-interest, where every man "must exist for his own sake, neither sacrificing himself to others nor others to himself." Politically, this means laissez-faire capitalism, a complete separation of government and economics, where the only purpose of government is to protect man's individual rights. In aesthetics, she wrote, art is a concretization of "metaphysical abstractions," and she defined a theory of "romantic realism."

Her means of conveying these ideas to the world were public speeches, radio and television appearances, private lectures and conversations; and later, through a new organization, a new periodical, and essay collections.

Her first speaking engagements on *Atlas Shrugged* came five months after its publication and were arranged by university students in New York City. In 1960 she lectured at Yale University on "Faith and Force: Destroyers of the Modern World," and then presented this and other talks before large audiences at Princeton, Columbia, Brown, and other universities. In her first presentation at Boston's Ford Hall Forum, she explained her willingness to address audiences of "liberals," i.e., her "antagonists":

> [I]n the 1930s I envied the "Liberals" for the fact that their leaders entered political campaigns armed not with worn-out bromides, but with intellectual arguments. I disagreed with everything they said, but I would have fought to the death for the method by which they said it: for an intellectual approach to political problems. . . As an advocate of reason, freedom, individualism, and capitalism, I seek to address myself to men of the intellect—wherever such may still be found—and I believe that more of them may be found among the former "liberals" than the present "conservatives."[5]

Through regular radio appearances, she considerably expanded her audience. In 1960, she delivered a series of four lectures on "Our Cultural Bankruptcy" over WBAI radio in New York City, and between 1962 and 1966 she presented three different series for WBAI and Columbia University's radio station.

Private discussion remained her preferred forum, as she often discussed her ideas with friends and associates until dawn. She continued teaching Objectivism to Leonard Peikoff, who received his

Rand on the set of CBS Television's "The Great Challenge," a Symposium on America's Continuing Revolution, March 1, 1962. Panelists (from left to right): James MacGregor Burns, Rand, David E. Lilienthal, Harry Ashmore and Russell Kirk. With his back to the camera is moderator Eric Severeid.

Ph.D. in philosophy in 1964, and she presented informal lectures on fiction and nonfiction in her apartment. In 1962 Nathaniel Branden, who had presented a lecture series on Objectivism in 1958 with Rand's editorial assistance, established Nathaniel Branden Institute, Inc. (NBI), offering "Basic Principles of Objectivism" as well as courses on psychology, economics, and philosophy presented by members of "the Collective" in New York City. In response to growing demand, NBI courses were tape recorded and replayed at gatherings around the world.

In 1961, Random House published *For the New Intellectual*, introducing Rand's philosophy in a nonfiction format for the first time to a wide audience. It was the first of seven nonfiction books she would write. In 1962 Rand established *The Objectivist Newsletter*, the first of three periodicals devoted to Objectivism and its application to modern culture, which changed to magazine format in 1967 under the title *The Objectivist*. These periodicals presented her new theoretical work, as well as contributions from psychologists, economists, historians, and other philosophers. Her own essays defined her views on such topics as antitrust laws, censorship, the nature of capi-

Rand's undated pencil drawing
of O'Connor

Three of the hundreds of notes Rand
("Fluff") and O'Connor ("Cubbyhole")
left for each other throughout the day,
ca. 1950s.

Cubbyhole!

Please wake me up at 8:30 a.m.

× × × × × × ×
× × × × × ×
× × × × × × A.

Dear Fluff.
Au Reservoir
(foreign for so long)
food premises
(not where your house
is but where your
mind is) xxx Oscar
cubby hole xxx × × ×

Ayn Darling.
Don't let "it"
get you down
today — keep a
stiff upper lip, or
shoot off your lips.
Wisdom of the sages
"Frankie" × × ×

Right *A Lester Kraus photograph for the paperback cover of* The Virtue of Selfishness, *1964.*

Below *Rand's revisions of advertising copy written by E. L. Doctorow, then an employee of Random House, in preparation for the publication of the 1963 paperback edition of* For the New Intellectual.

```
COVER FOUR                    FOR THE NEW INTELLECTUAL


AYN RAND CHALLENGES                            USE LARGE PHOTO
the prevalent philosophical doctrines of
The fundamentals of today's                          OF

dominant theories and the                       AYN RAND

"atmosphere of guilt, of

panic, of despair, of bore-

dom and of all-pervasive

evasion," which they have

created.
```

talism, the nature of art, and the moral basis for the right to abortion.

New American Library published several anthologies of these articles, beginning with *The Virtue of Selfishness: A New Concept of Egoism* (1964), then *Capitalism: The Unknown Ideal* (1966). Also in 1967, The Objectivist, Inc. published *Introduction to Objectivist*

Ilona Royce-Smithkin, Portrait of Ayn Rand, an oil painting on canvas, 1965, featured on many paperback editions in the 1970s. After first seeing the painting, Rand, according to the artist, said: "This is exactly how I feel about myself."

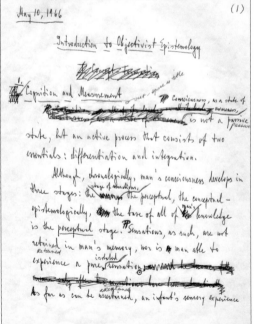

Manuscript page from Introduction to Objectivist Epistemology

IN PERSON

Nash Productions presents the author of 'Atlas Shrugged,'
'The Fountainhead' and 'For the New Intellectual'

AYN RAND

on 'America's Persecuted Minority: Big Business.'
Ayn Rand will also answer questions from the audience.

SUN · SEPT 29 · 8 PM
McCORMICK PLACE

Arie Crown Theater. All seats reserved; $3.50 each; ten for $30.
Some main floor seats are still available . Send order by mail now.
Nash Productions, Room 1336 A, 55 East Washington · CE 6-4241

MAIL TO: NASH PRODUCTIONS, 55 E. WASHINGTON, CHICAGO 2, ILL.
Please send the tickets indicated below for Ayn Rand's September 29th talk
at McCormick Place. $........check payable to Nash Productions is enclosed.
_____Tickets at $3.50 each   _____Tickets at ten for $30.00

PRINT NAME

CAPACITY LIMITED

ADDRESS

CITY   ZONE   STATE

ALL SEATS RESERVED

TICKETS ISSUED IN ORDER OF RECEIPT · PLEASE MAIL PROMPTLY

Promotional material for Rand's talk,
"America's Most Persecuted Minority:
Big Business," attended by an audience
of 2,500 at Chicago's McCormick Place,
September 29, 1963.

Epistemology, a work on the nature of concept formation.

Slowly, Rand's work attracted the notice of contemporary academics. She was invited to several forums and symposiums, first as a visitor and then as a participant. In May 1961 she attended talks by Noam Chomsky, Sidney Hook, and Nelson Goodman at a Conference on Methods in Philosophy and the Sciences at Brooklyn College. In October 1962 she presented a paper, "Art as Sense of Life," at the annual meeting of the American Society for Aesthetics at Harvard University. She also corresponded and discussed philosophy with John Hospers and Martin Lean, and she met with John Herman Randall and Brand Blanshard after expressing enthusiasm for aspects of their work. However, the gulf between Rand's methodology and context and those of contemporary academic philosophy made a true rapport all but impossible. Rand's project of providing a comprehensive and integrated view of existence and of man's relationship to existence was considered irrelevant. The academy did not know what to make of her: she was an individualist but not a subjectivist or skeptic; she was an absolutist but not a dogmatist.

But outside of academia, Rand was becoming a media phenomenon. She was interviewed by *Playboy* magazine in March 1964 and was a guest on numerous television shows, including three times in 1967 on *The Tonight Show Starring Johnny Carson.*

Ouray, Colorado. Rand chose this town in the Rocky Mountains as the location for the fictional Galt's Gulch in Atlas Shrugged. She and O'Connor visited Ouray on a research trip in 1948, "falling in love" with the town, and returned there on a 1966 vacation.

Right One of a series of billboards placed throughout the South by a young Ted Turner, through Turner Advertising, "to create more interest in Miss Rand's works," 1967

Nevertheless, she remained an unassuming woman, who preferred one-on-one conversations to public appearances. She was generous with her time, eager for philosophical discussion, gracious and intellectually witty, possessed of an unbending resolve and an electrifying temperament.

Nevertheless, acceptance within the intellectual establishment remained elusive. The major intellectual publications, both liberal and conservative, increasingly ignored her nonfiction books, until reviews nearly ceased to appear at all. Still, Rand refused to disappear. The public discussed her and bought her books as never

O'Connor's painting Man Also Rises, *used for the dust jacket of the 25th anniversary edition of* The Fountainhead. *The painting, she wrote, "represents Frank's version of a sunrise we once saw in San Francisco."* [6]

before. However, the mainstream press noted the phenomenon she had become, criticizing her novels as "soapboxes" for her philosophical agenda, the ideas themselves as "simplistic," and increasingly, with character attacks, labeling her an "authoritarian" or "impossible."

By the late 1960s, NBI had expanded as an educational organization: in addition to courses attended by thousands, it maintained an extensive book service. However, at the peak of NBI's success, relations between Rand and Nathaniel Branden deteriorated. Their relationship had evolved over eighteen years, from intellectual associates to close personal friends and professional allies. For a period of several years in the 1950s, and with the consent of their spouses, they had had a romantic affair, which ended probably near the time of the publication of *Atlas Shrugged*. Their association continued for another ten years until she ended it in 1968. She presented her reasons in the May 1968 issue of *The Objectivist*; among the underlying causes, she wrote, were a series of deceptions, including Branden's failure to practice the philosophy he was teaching his students.

The organization was gone, but Ayn Rand was not. She remained at her desk, thinking and writing, her lifelong leitmotifs of the "unusual" and "reason" undiminished, the world outside her study still able to inspire her to pause, put down her pen, and look up.

Lift-off of Apollo 11, *Cape Kennedy, July 21, 1969*

"In His Own Image"
1969–1982

> It began with a large patch of bright yellow orange flame, shooting
> sideways from under the base of the rocket. . . . In the next instant the
> flame and the rocket were hidden by such a sweep of dark red fire. . . .
> The dark red fire parted into two gigantic wings, as if a hydrant were
> shooting streams of fire outward and up, toward the zenith—and
> between the two wings, against a pitch-black sky, the rocket rose slow-
> ly, so slowly that it seemed to hang still in the air, a pale cylinder with
> a blinding oval of white light at the bottom.
>
> Ayn Rand, "Apollo 11"[1]

Along with other notable Americans, Rand was invited by
NASA to attend the historic launch of *Apollo 11*. It was now twelve
years since the publication of *Atlas Shrugged*, and the invitation
was another sign of her growing recognition. But more important-
ly to Rand, the launch was an opportunity to write about a truly
great contemporary event—not an imaginary event, conceived in
fiction to portray that world as it *should* be, but a real event as it
actually happened. For Rand the landing of a manned spacecraft
on the moon was as an example of man's power to command
nature, but the event held an even deeper meaning to her, as she
described what she witnessed at Cape Kennedy as "the con-
cretized abstraction of man's greatness," an "unmistakably
human" event, "with 'human,' for once, meaning *grandeur*."

The moon landing was a scientific milestone and a magnificent
demonstration of the practical application of reason. However,
throughout the tumultuous 1960s, Rand had targeted—both in her
writing and public speeches—movements and organizations she
identified as fundamentally *ir*rational. Irrationality, she concluded
had become a force of its own, and in her essays Rand relentlessly

Ayn Rand knows that a real revolution starts in men's minds, not in the streets.

Through her books, millions have discovered how Ayn Rand cuts through convention and cliché to get down to the basic meaning of life. If revolution means real change, a liberation of the mind, Ayn Rand is a revolutionary force without peer. NAL is proud to publish four seminal works by this major writer and thinker.

THE VIRTUE OF SELFISHNESS
The famous ethical system that holds reason as man's means of survival—and upholds a man's right to exist for his own sake. $4.50

CAPITALISM: THE UNKNOWN IDEAL
A challenging presentation of the thesis that "capitalism is not merely the 'practical,' but the only *moral* system in history." $6.50

THE ROMANTIC MANIFESTO
Ayn Rand's personal artistic credo—a new theory of esthetics—and a devastating critique of modern art $5.95

NIGHT OF JANUARY 16TH
This famous play is an engrossing example of the Randian literary technique: a melodrama integrated with a philosophical message. $5.00

NAL
TIMES MIRROR
NEW AMERICAN LIBRARY

Distributed by W. W. Norton & Company, Inc.
55 Fifth Avenue, New York, New York 10003

MERIDIAN 🔟

AYN RAND
THE NEW LEFT:
THE ANTI-INDUSTRIAL
REVOLUTION

REVISED AND UPDATED TO INCLUDE
THE AGE OF ENVY

Above *Cover for* The New Left:
The Anti-Industrial Revolution,
designed by R. Heinsdal

Left *New American Library advertisement
for four Rand books,* Publishers Weekly,
August 9, 1971

attacked it wherever she deemed it had manifested itself—from the student rebellion to the environmentalist movement. She wrote that the student movement of the 1960s tried to legitimize the initiation of physical force, and that the environmentalist movement was nothing less than "the anti-industrial revolution" guided by a basic hatred of Western civilization.[2]

In the 1960s Rand conducted "The Objectivist Workshops," including four all-day sessions covering aspects of her theory of concept formation. Attending was a group of professors and graduate students in philosophy and cognate fields. She continued to write essays for *The Objectivist*, many of which were later anthologized into such books as *The Romantic Manifesto: A Philosophy of Literature* (1969) and *The New Left: The Anti-Industrial Revolution* (1971). However, publishing the monthly magazine became onerous, as Rand not only had to write her own articles but to heavily edit submissions from less experienced contributors as well. In the hope of easing her editorial burden, she began a second series of lectures on nonfiction writing, asking her students to approach writing as a profession, not as a duty to a cause.

Hoping to expand her audience further, Rand closed *The Objectivist* monthly in 1971 and began issuing *The Ayn Rand Letter*, a philosophical newsletter covering a range of topics—from Watergate and the Vietnam War to the theories of psychologist B. F. Skinner and philosopher John Rawls. The newsletter was published bi-weekly, and eighty-one issues appeared overall. In conjunction with the launch of *The Ayn Rand Letter*, Rand renewed her

ДЕКАБРЬ 1971 / № 182 • 50 коп.

Америка

воинами страдании», — говорит он.

АЙН РЭНД

Писательница, поборница консерватизма

Айн Рэнд, женщина открыто и безоговорочно высказывающая свои взгляды, изложила их со всей силой убеждения в двух имевших большой успех романах и в довольно резкой консервативной философской системе, которую она и ее последователи считают панацеей от всех зол, встречающихся в обществе. Айн Рэнд стала известна в 1943 году, когда был опубликован ее полный динамики роман «Родник», в котором описывается блестящий волевой архитектор, взрывающий спроектированный им жилой комплекс, чтобы не допустить в нем переделок. Недоброжелательные отзывы критики вызвали интерес к роману, и книга стала быстро расходиться. Во втором ее бестселлере «Атлас пожал плечами» (1957) описывается хаос, происшедший в Америке, когда ведущие ученые и директора коммерческих предприятий объявили забастовку в знак протеста против того, что они вынуждены нести бремя ответственности за все общество, не пользуясь при этом должным уважением.

Читателям произведений Айн Рэнд, все еще покупающим ежегодно по 100 000 экземпляров ее книг, нравится не только драматическая фабула, но и горячность взглядов, пространно излагаемых ее героями и героинями. Интерес, проявленный читателями, побудил Айн Рэнд систематизировать свои воззрения под общим названием «объективизм». Свою теорию она развивает в выступлениях и в курсе лекций в Институте имени Натаниэла Брэндена.

Окончив Ленинградский университет, она в 1926 году эмигрировала в Америку и прямо отправилась в Голливуд, где сперва была статистом, а потом киносценаристом. «Первый же мой сценарий был принят, — вспоминает она. — Как и моя первая пьеса и мой первый роман». Но имя ее оставалось неизвестным до выхода в свет «Родника», к написанию которого она готовилась, работая бесплатно машинисткой в конторе одного нью-йоркского архитектора.

Айн Рэнд уже 42 года замужем за Фрэнком О'Коннором, бывшим актером, с которым она познакомилась в Голливуде. «Фрэнк наглядный пример того, — объясняет писательница, — что люди, которых я описываю, действительно существуют в реальной жизни». Супруги живут в Нью-Йорке.

ГЭС ХОЛЛ

Генеральный секретарь
Коммунистической партии США

«Я впитал социализм с молоком матери», — говорит Гэс Холл, генеральный секретарь Коммунистической партии США, крупный шестидесятилетний мужчина. Он родился в горах Месаби, в шахтерском городке в Миннесоте. У него девять братьев и сестер. Его родители Мэтт и Сусанн Холберг, иммигранты из Финляндии, были членами-основателями Коммунистической партии США. Гэс Холл (сокративший впоследствии свою фамилию) стал членом Коммунистической партии в 17 лет. Когда ему исполнился 21 год, он поехал в СССР, где в Москве два года изучал теорию марксизма-ленинизма. По возвращении в США он стал принимать актив-

«Я твердо — без сомнений, без исключений, без всяких оговорок — верю в то, что свобода слова означает только одно: не твори ничего людям за их взгляды, которых они придерживаются, за убеждения, которые они высказывают, за речи, которые они произносят».
Судья Хьюго Л. Блэк

*Clipping from the December 1971 issue of Amerika magazine seen in
Leningrad by Rand's sister, Nora, leading to their reunion in April 1974.*

effort to promote her books, appearing in print ads and a television commercial for the *New York Daily News*. She was inundated with speaking invitations, but accepted only a few, among them her annual talk at Boston's Ford Hall Forum, which she considered the most intellectually honest venue in the United States. She also accepted an invitation from the United States Military Academy at West Point, where her talk bore the title, "Philosophy: Who Needs It."

By the early 1970s, Rand had achieved the goal she set for herself while still a child in Russia. She was addressing the world as a novelist-philosopher. She was famous on an international level; except, of course, in her native country.

In late 1972, at a Leningrad exhibit sponsored by the United States Information Agency, a sixty-two-year-old woman read the December 1971 issue of *America Illustrated* magazine and discovered a picture and profile on Ayn Rand. The woman was Eleanora Drobysheva, Rand's youngest sister, presumed dead and now the only surviving member of her immediate family. A correspondence between Nora and Rand led to their reunion in New York City in 1974. After a separation of forty-six years, what began as a joyous occasion turned, sadly, into a realization of an unbridgeable personal distance, for they no longer shared important values. Nora disliked her sister's works and philosophy, and after a short stay, she voluntarily returned to the Soviet Union.

At around the same time, Rand's health began to decline.

Nora (left) with unidentified woman, ca. 1973

After decades of heavy smoking, she was diagnosed with lung cancer, and surgery to remove part of her lung left her weakened. She was able to regain some of her strength after convalescing, but her husband had fallen ill in the meantime and required medical care.

Rand, O'Connor, President Gerald Ford, Alan Greenspan, and his mother, at Greenspan's swearing-in ceremony as Chairman of the Council of Economic Advisors, September 4, 1974

Despite their health problems, Rand and O'Connor made two trips to the White House during the Ford administration. In 1974 they attended Alan Greenspan's swearing-in ceremony as the Chairman of the Council of Economic Advisors, and in 1976, they returned as guests at a state dinner honoring Australian Prime Minister Malcolm Fraser, a noted admirer of *Atlas Shrugged*.

In 1976, Rand's career as a writer of nonfiction was in its second decade. Her books were in university libraries across the world, translated into fifteen languages, and read by millions, yet her work still garnered scant attention from academic philosophers. With few exceptions, her views were not included in the scholarly debate, either in college courses or academic publications.

Now seventy-one years old, she had lived a public life that few had witnessed closely from its start. The exception was her husband Frank. Although he was not a philosopher, he did share her deepest values and approach to life. A self-contained man, he had pursued his interests in acting as well as art and design. His work in floral and landscape design had evolved into a serious interest in drawing and painting. His art was a visual complement to his wife's novels, and she described the spirit of his paintings as "laughter let loose in the universe."[3]

After completing *Atlas Shrugged*—and occasionally over the next eight years—Rand made notes for a new novel whose theme was unrequited love, but the project went no further. She later accounted for her withdrawal from fiction writing, stating that "it is impossible to write about heroic characters or a romantic story in today's setting. The world is in such a low state that I could not bear to put it in fiction."[4] She thought about several historical and futuristic novels with philosophical themes, but none was ever begun.

By 1976 she could no longer meet the demands of her bi-weekly newsletter. She closed *The Ayn Rand Letter*, wishing to return full-time to writing philosophy and no longer willing to comment on contemporary culture, which she considered repugnant. In an interview for *Time* magazine, she said: "I am haunted by a quotation from Nietzsche: 'It is not my function to be a flyswatter.'"[5] Before closing *The Ayn Rand Letter*, she was able to announce an important event, which began the safe transfer of her philosophical legacy: a course on the entire theoretical structure of Objectivism, offered by Leonard

From the proof sheet of photographs later used for the cover of Leonard Peikoff's Objectivism: the Philosophy of Ayn Rand *(1991), based on his 1976 course*

(March 31, 1967)

"Siegfried"

Greatest motion picture ever produced (Movies are a visual-dramatic medium, an art of telling a story by visual means.)

Specifically — esthetic greatness, the best use of the medium. In movies, the story determines the "what" — the direction determines the "how."

This is strictly a director's picture. The director is the stylist of a movie. (The director was Fritz Lang — who was the first genius of this new medium and, so far, the best.)

What to look for: stylized purposefulness — ... the essentials of every aspect are caught to look for. The forest, or the castle) — there are no irrelevant or accidental touches, everything is consciously calculated, even the movements of the actors — ... — the difference between "artificial" and "stylized" — not nothing is artificially stilted ...

— any frame can be ... All exteriors were done in studio. have the composition of a painting ... The slogan: "Nothing in this film is accidental."

The story: malevolent universe and anti-sex. Psychologically, villainous, should have been the heroine of the story ...

Rand's March 31, 1967, notes on the film Die Nibelungen: Siegfried, which, she wrote, was "as close to a great work of art as the films have yet come." (Romantic Manifesto, p. 72). Director Fritz Lang, with whom she spoke on the telephone in 1974, was her first choice to direct Atlas Shrugged.

Georg August Koch as Hildebrand in
Die Nibelungen: Siegfried (1924).
From Rand's postcards collected in Berlin, 1926.

Peikoff. Though no longer motivated to write a treatise on her philosophy, Rand was inspired by the opportunity to oversee a course taught by her best student, to whom she had been privately teaching Objectivism for twenty-five years.

As she concluded *The Ayn Rand Letter,* she left her readers with a valedictory in which she considered her origins and the state of the fight for individual rights. She remembered once saying that she concerned herself with politics to reach the day when she would not have to be concerned with politics. That day never arrived. The public voice defending reason and freedom, one she had sought after desperately since her days in Russia, turned out—much to her surprise—to be her own voice. This was, she wrote, "an admission of a sort I don't like to make: a complaint. . . . I did not want, intend or expect to be the only philosophical defender of man's rights in the country of man's rights. But if I am, I am."[6]

On a hopeful note, she thought there were faint signs that the world was reconsidering its politics—by considering *her* politics. She stated emphatically that the political ascendancy of Ronald Reagan, whose incorporation of religion into politics and opposition to abortion were anathema to Rand, was not a sign that a defender of individual rights had emerged. Neither was the development of the libertarian movement, which she maintained plagiarized her ideas and held philosophy in contempt. Yet there were some faint signs that her name was being openly and unashamedly linked to public figures leading the fight against the welfare state, such as British Prime Minister Margaret Thatcher and Australian Prime Minister Malcolm Fraser. "I can at least proudly say that I had some part in [the turn to the right]. I gave a moral foundation to a free society, to capitalism."[7]

With the closing of *The Ayn Rand Letter*, Rand began reconsidering her professional future. She had planned to expand her theory of knowledge, and she envisioned integrating neurology, epistemology, and mathematics into one unified theory. Her notes on this remained fragmentary, and she never developed these ideas systematically. Her major personal preoccupation throughout this time was caring for her ailing husband.

For recreation, she listened to her "tiddly-wink" music—turn-of-the-century one-steps, cakewalks, and ragtime compositions—as well as classical music. She watched television shows, including the original *Perry Mason* and *Charlie's Angels*, as well as telecasts of her favorite films and operas. She amassed a collection of 50,000 stamps, attended philatelic shows with friends, and even wrote an essay, "Why I Like Stamp Collecting," for a leading stamp journal. But her greatest "recreation" was discussing philosophy. New and old friends visited regularly for the kind of serious conversation she loved, and occasionally for the kind of spirited party she enjoyed. Arline Mann, a young acquaintance, recalled such a time:

> It could possibly have been her 50th anniversary party. She was playing some music and people were dancing. And for some reason, I decided to do some sort of cakewalk, where you put one leg out in front of the other very stiffly. She was very taken with this and wanted me to keep doing it. A line formed. And she was delighted to have people doing this little cakewalk right around her living room.[8]

In November 1979, after a long illness, Frank O'Connor died. Rand and O'Connor had been married fifty years. The special visibility and inspiration he provided for her was now a memory. In the period following his death, she was terribly depressed; initially, nothing interested her. She had lost her "top value," but, as she said on national television, she still loved "the world in general and I do love ideas. . . . and I do love man."[9]

Earlier that year Rand had become a philosophical consultant for a new publication, *The Objectivist Forum*, edited by Harry Binswanger. She also assisted editorially at the start of his proposed lexicon of Objectivist terms. In 1980, she wrote an introduction to "the first work by an Objectivist philosopher other than myself." The book, *The Ominous Parallels: The End of Freedom in America* by Leonard Peikoff, presented the Objectivist philosophy of history, analyzing the causes of National Socialism and the philosophic parallels between pre-Nazi Germany and contemporary America. "If you like my works, you will like this book," she wrote in its introduction.[10]

"We were really, I would say, spiritually collaborators. I have always told him I could not have written without him. He denies it; he thinks I would have broken through, but I know too well, and perhaps that's the only tribute I can pay him with my readers, that it is impossible to hold a benevolent universe view consistently, the way I had to hold it to write what I have written, and to project an ideal life, when the actual life around us was getting worse and worse; when it was all going in the direction of Ellsworth Toohey, and I was writing about John Galt. I couldn't have done it if it weren't for the fact that I knew one person who did live up to my heroes and my view of life. He gave me the benevolent universe that I write about, and that is how we combined. We were married over 50 years."[11] Julius Shulman's photograph of Rand and O'Connor at the Chatsworth ranch, 1947.

Despite her husband's recent death, Rand was revitalized by another "new assignment." Her spirit and creative ambitions revived slowly as she turned her attention to a film adaptation of *Atlas Shrugged*. There had been a long history of failed attempts to develop and finance a film, including efforts involving producer

Albert S. Ruddy, the NBC television network, and Stanley and Michael Jaffe. In unpublished notes from the 1970s, she had assessed the pros and cons of working once again in Hollywood:

Pro (the advantages of having [Atlas Shrugged] produced.)		Con (Without my okay)	
1.	Money	1.	Doesn't matter.
2.	Augmented sale of book.	2.	Maybe hurt by bad movie
3.	Political impact	3.	Will be bad—necessarily.
4.	Excitement of working on it.	4.	Will be unspeakable torture.
5.	My fame and reputation.	5.	Maybe destroyed

After the grueling experience of adapting *The Fountainhead*, she vowed never to adapt another one of her books for the screen unless she had a financial emergency. However, by the 1970s, she became interested enough in the project to consider supervising the work of another writer, and, during this period, she considered the qualities such a writer might need:

I want "AS" produced for TV—I do not want a "Comedia del Arte" scenario for improvisation. Today's "inspirational" school of writing & directing (and acting)—"AS" cannot be done that way—(I know what drama, movies and TV)—(Any one who is afraid of me, is not competent to deal with the book)—(What can they offer me?)[12]

At this stage, what Hollywood could offer was a talented screenwriter, Sterling Silliphant, whose *In the Heat of the Night* Rand admired. A television production, she said, would "make the ideas more vivid. More dramatic. . . . a perfect vehicle to concretize the meaning of the book's events."[13] However, due to a change of administration at NBC, the television miniseries in development was canceled.

Despite her disappointment, Rand remained interested in bringing *Atlas Shrugged* to the screen. In early 1981 she discovered a television actor whose qualities revived her interest in the film project. The actor, Hans Gudegast (or Eric Braeden, as he became known on American television) became for her the cinematic

Right *A section from Rand's notes on a film schedule and possible actors for prospective miniseries of* Atlas Shrugged, *September 16–17, 1978*

Below *Photo of Rand in New York City's Grand Central terminal. From* "Ayn Rand Returns," Look *magazine's April 14, 1979, article about a prospective miniseries of* Atlas Shrugged. *Photo by Theo Westenberger*

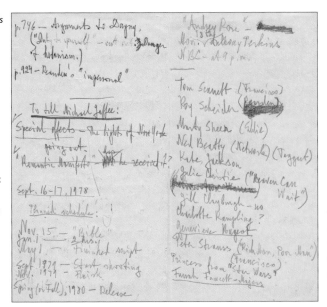

embodiment of her *Atlas* character Francisco d'Anconia. Although she never contacted Gudegast, she proceeded with the idea of creating the proper role for him, in effect, to save him from parts she thought beneath his ability. Although she gradually changed her mind about his suitability, Gudegast was the spiritual catalyst for a project that revived her own spirits: she began writing a teleplay of *Atlas Shrugged*—her first fiction in nearly twenty years. By the end of 1981, she had written nearly one-third of her script. Although her energy had diminished since Frank's death, the challenge of writing the screenplay gradually engaged her. She felt that in her hand, the assignment would not be a rehash of old work, but a new effort in the "technological radiance" of a medium she loved.[14]

In 1981 Rand was invited by James U. Blanchard III of the National Committee for Monetary Reform to deliver a speech at his November monetary conference in New Orleans. Her days of public speaking had passed, and she was uncomfortable with flying, but Blanchard offered to transport her to New Orleans in a private rail car and to pay for her appearance in gold coins. Delighted by his offer, she was unable to resist.

Rand and a small group of friends departed from New York City's Pennsylvania Station and traveled to New Orleans. In her November 1981 speech, "The Sanction of the Victims," she attacked businessmen for financing universities that advocate the destruction of capitalism. At the end of her speech, she changed the topic from university to Hollywood finance. After explaining that a "distinguished producer" had tried but failed to make a television miniseries or theatrical film of her novel, *Atlas Shrugged*, she announced:

> Allow me to say, even though I do not like to say it, that if there existed a novel of the same value and popularity as Atlas Shrugged, but written to glorify collectivism (which would be a contradiction in terms), it would have been produced on the screen long ago.

The last published photograph taken of Rand, delivering her talk "The Sanction of the Victims," New Orleans, November 21, 1981.

But I do not believe in giving up—and so, in answer to many questions, I chose this occasion to make a very special announcement:

I am writing a nine-hour teleplay for Atlas Shrugged.
I intend to produce the mini-series myself.[15]

The audience rose in a body and cheered. At the age of seventy-six, Rand not only intended to produce the series on her own, she was already planning her return to Hollywood to personally oversee all phases of the film's production.

She left New Orleans and returned to New York City to resume work on several projects: the film production, a new anthology of essays to be titled "Philosophy: Who Needs It," and a revision of her New Orleans talk for her April 1982 appearance at Boston's Ford Hall Forum.

The New Orleans speech was to be her last public appearance, however. On her way home, she became ill and remained so throughout December. In accordance with an old Russian custom—doing on New Year's Day what one planned to do throughout the year—she summoned the energy to write at her desk on January 1, 1982. It was a portion of her *Atlas Shrugged* teleplay: the scene involved Dagny Taggart and Hank Rearden on their morning together following the triumphant opening of the John Galt railroad line. The scene begins with Dagny awakening, in bed, in a light-filled room, watching someone off screen, smiling in acknowledgement of the previous night—it was the last fiction she was ever to write.

In January 1982 her health declined rapidly and she was hospitalized with pulmonary problems. From her hospital bed, she made final arrangements for her new book and discussed the possibility of addressing the Ford Hall Forum during her convalescence via long-distance telephone hook-up. When it became clear that no recovery was possible, she asked to return to her apartment, where she died on March 6, 1982. At her funeral, more than 800 people paid their final respects, while "tiddly-wink" recordings honored her life. The next day— following a reading of Kipling's poem "If"—she was buried alongside her husband.

Epilogue

In 1936 Ayn Rand wrote that if her life could have a theme song, its title would be "individualism." By the end of her life, her song had become a symphony of philosophy: its five movements were the nature of the universe, of reason, of the good, of government, and of art.

Her novels and their heroes continue to attract new readers. She explained this appeal in the 1968 preface to *The Fountainhead*. "[T]he best of mankind's youth," she wrote, start life with

> *an undefined sense of enormous expectation, the sense that one's life is important, that great achievements are within one's capacity, and that great things lie ahead.*
>
> *It is not in the nature of man—nor of any living entity—to start out by giving up, by spitting in one's own face and damning existence. . . . Some give up at the first touch of pressure; some sell out; some run down by imperceptible degrees and lose their fire, never knowing when or how they lose it. Then all of these vanish in the vast swamp of their elders who tell them persistently that maturity consists of abandoning one's mind; security, of abandoning one's values; practicality, of losing self-esteem. Yet a few hold on and move on, knowing that the fire is not to be betrayed, learning how to give it shape, purpose and reality. But whatever their future, at the dawn of their lives, men seek a noble vision of man's nature and of life's potential.*
>
> *There are very few guideposts to find.* The Fountainhead *is one of them.*
>
> *That is one of the cardinal reasons of* The Fountainhead's *lasting appeal: it is the confirmation of the spirit of youth, proclaiming man's glory, showing how much is possible.*

It does not matter that only a few in each generation will grasp and achieve the full reality of man's proper stature—and that the rest will betray it. It is those few that move the world and give life its meaning—and it is those few that I have always sought to address.[1]

References

Looking Out
1. This and subsequent quotations are from unpublished interviews conducted by Barbara and Nathaniel Branden between December 1960 and May 1961.
2. "To the Readers of *The Fountainhead*," *Letters of Ayn Rand*, Appendix.

Important Things
1. *The Romantic Manifesto*, p. 4–5
2. *Introduction to The Fountainhead*, p. ix

Freedom to Write
1. *Letters of Ayn Rand*, p. 2
2. *Facets of Ayn Rand*, p. iii
3. *Journals of Ayn Rand*, p. 48
4. *For the New Intellectual*, p. 60
5. From the 1968 introduction to *Night of January 16th* p. 2

The Ideal
1. *For the New Intellectual*, p. 25
2. *New York Herald-Tribune*, June 29, 1941
3. *The Fountainhead*, p. 606
4. *Journals of Ayn Rand*, p. 77
5. *For the New Intellectual*, p. 68
6. *Letters of Ayn Rand*, p. 92
7. *The Early Ayn Rand*, p. 293
8. *Letters of Ayn Rand*, p. 44

The Real
1. *Letters of Ayn Rand*, p. 54
2. *Letters of Ayn Rand*, p. 74
3. *Letters of Ayn Rand*, p. 54

4. *Letters of Ayn Rand*, p. 492
5. *Letters of Ayn Rand*, p. 112
6. *Letters of Ayn Rand*, p. 113
7. *Letters of Ayn Rand*, p. 106
8. *Journals of Ayn Rand*, p. 382
9. *Letters of Ayn Rand*, p. 418
10. *Ayn Rand: A Sense of Life*, p. 168
11. *Letters of Ayn Rand*, p. 117
12. *The Virtue of Selfishness*, p. 84
13. *Letters of Ayn Rand*, p. 390
14. *Letters of Ayn Rand*, p. 214

The Strike
1. *For the New Intellectual*, p. 88
2. *Who is Ayn Rand?*, p. 167

A Philosophy for Living on Earth
1 *The Early Ayn Rand*, p. 246
2. *The Romantic Manifesto*
3. *The Voice of Reason*, p. 18
4. "Introducing Objectivism," *Los Angeles Times*, June 17, 1962
5. *The Voice of Reason*, p. 86
6. *Introduction to The Fountainhead,* p. vii

"In His Own Image"
1. *The Voice of Reason*, p. 165
2. *Return of the Primitive*, pp. 27, 270
3. *Ayn Rand: A Sense of Life*, p. 145
4. Ford Hall Forum Q & A, 1977
5. *The Ayn Rand Letter*, p. 382
6. *The Ayn Rand Letter*, p. 363
7. *The Objectivist Forum*, August 1980, p. 1
8. Arline Mann (1996)
9. *Ayn Rand: A Sense of Life*, p. 182
10. *The Ominous Parallels*, p. 9
11. "Objective Communication" course; Q & A, 1980.
12. *Ayn Rand Papers*
13. *The Objectivist Forum*, August 1980, p. 1
14. *The Romantic Manifesto*, p. 76
15. *The Voice of Reason*, p. 145

Epilogue
1. *The Fountainhead*, 1968, p. xi

Chronology

1905   Born in St. Petersburg on February 2 (January 20 on the Julian calendar).

1912   Family moves to apartment on Znamenskaya Square.

1917   Start of 1917 Russian revolution. Bolsheviks seize power on October 25.

1918   To escape civil war, family moves to Ukraine and then to Yevpatoria, in the Crimea.

1921   Graduates from Yevpatoria High School #4. Family returns to Petrograd. Enrolls in Petrograd State University.

1924   Graduates from Leningrad State University. Enrolls in State Technicum for Screen Arts.

1925   First known publication, "Pola Negri" pamphlet, published (unattributed) in USSR. Receives permission to leave USSR.

1926   "Hollywood: American City of Movies" pamphlet published in USSR. Departs Leningrad and travels to Chicago. Moves to Hollywood. Meets Cecil B. DeMille, who hires her as movie extra on *The King of Kings*. Meets her future husband, Frank O'Connor.

1927   Hired by DeMille as junior screenwriter.

1929   Marries Frank O'Connor. Hired by RKO Pictures wardrobe department.

1931	Becomes U.S. citizen.
1932	Sells "Red Pawn" treatment to Universal Pictures.
1934	Writes "Ideal." First play, *Woman on Trial* (aka *Night of January 16th*), opens in Hollywood.
	Moves to New York City.
1935	Makes first notes for *The Fountainhead. Night of January 16th* opens on Broadway.
1936	*We the Living* published in United States and England.
1938	*Anthem* published in England.
1940	*The Unconquered* (her adaptation of *We the Living*) opens on Broadway.
1943	*The Fountainhead* published. Begins writing "The Moral Basis of Individualism" (unfinished). Moves to California to write screenplay for *The Fountainhead*.
1944	Purchases the von Sternberg House designed by Richard Neutra. Hired by Hal Wallis and writes screenplay for *Love Letters*.
1945	Makes first notes for *Atlas Shrugged. The Fountainhead* reaches #6 on the *New York Times* bestseller list. First installment of the "illustrated" *Fountainhead* published in Hearst newspapers nationwide.
1946	First U.S. edition of *Anthem* published. Joins Motion Picture Alliance for the Preservation of American Ideals, which later publishes her "Screen Guide for Americans."
1947	Testifies on Communist influence in Hollywood before House Un-American Activities Committee.
1949	*The Fountainhead* film released.
1951	Moves permanently to New York City.

1952	"The Collective" begins meeting.
1955	Finishes writing "Galt's Speech."
1957	Finishes writing *Atlas Shrugged*. *Atlas Shrugged* published.
1958	Gives private course on fiction writing. Presents first campus talk, at Queens College in New York City.
1960	Delivers first major campus talk, "Faith and Force: Destroyers of the Modern World," at Yale University.
1961	*For the New Intellectual* published. Presents first Ford Hall Forum talk.
1962	First issue of *The Objectivist Newsletter* published. Nathaniel Branden Institute opens. Weekly column begins in the *Los Angeles Times*.
1963	Receives honorary doctorate from Lewis and Clark University.
1964	*The Virtue of Selfishness* published.
1966	First installment of *Introduction to Objectivist Epistemology* published in *The Objectivist*. *Capitalism: The Unknown Ideal* published.
1967	Makes first appearance on *The Tonight Show Starring Johnny Carson*.
1969	*The Romantic Manifesto* published. Begins teaching nonfiction writing course.
1971	*The New Left: The Anti-Industrial Revolution* published.
1974	Presents "Philosophy: Who Needs It" talk at West Point.
1976	Publishes last article in *The Ayn Rand Letter*.
1979	*Introduction to Objectivist Epistemology* published by New American Library. Frank O'Connor dies.

| 1981 | Delivers last public lecture, "The Sanction of the Victims," in New Orleans. |
| 1982 | Dies in New York City on March 6. |

Bibliography

This bibliography lists works either cited or used in the research for this volume.

WORKS BY RAND

FICTION

Anthem (London: Cassell, 1938; rev. edition, Los Angeles: Pamphleteers, 1946; 3d ed., New York: Penguin, 1995).

Atlas Shrugged (New York: Random House, 1957).

The Fountainhead (Indianapolis: Bobbs-Merrill, 1943 and 1968).

Night of January 16th (New York: New American Library, 1968).

We the Living (New York: Macmillan, 1936; 2d ed., New York: Random House, 1959).

NONFICTION

Capitalism: The Unknown Ideal (New York: New American Library, 1966 and 1967).

For the New Intellectual (New York: Random House, 1961).

Introduction to Objectivist Epistemology (New York: The Objectivist Inc., 1967; 2d ed., New York: Penguin, 1990).

The New Left: The Anti-Industrial Revolution (New York: New American Library, 1971); rev. ed., New York: New American Library, 1975; retitled *Return of the Primitive*, New York: Penguin, 1999).

Philosophy: Who Needs It (New York: Bobbs-Merrill, 1982).

The Romantic Manifesto (New York: World Publishing, 1969; 2nd ed., New York: New American Library, 1971).

The Virtue of Selfishness (New York: New American Library, 1964).

PERIODICALS
Edited by Ayn Rand

The Objectivist Newsletter (1962–1965).
The Objectivist (1966–1971).
The Ayn Rand Letter (1971–1976).

SCREENPLAYS

"The Crying Sisters," adapted from *The Crying Sisters* by Mabel Seeley (New York: Grosset and Dunlap, 1939), Hal Wallis Productions, 1945, unproduced.

The Fountainhead, dir. King Vidor, perf. Gary Cooper, Patricia Neal and Raymond Massey, Warner Bros., 1949.

"House of Mist," adapted from *House of Mist* by Maria Luisa Bombal (New York: Farrar, Strauss and Co., 1947), Hal Wallis Productions, 1947, unproduced.

Love Letters, adapted from *The Love Letters* by Chris Massie (New York: Grosset and Dunlap, 1944), dir. William Dieterle, perf. Jennifer Jones and Joseph Cotton, Paramount Pictures, 1945.

"Red Pawn," Universal Pictures, 1932, unproduced.

You Came Along, with Robert Smith, adapted from "You Came Along" by Robert Smith, dir. John Farrow, perf. Robert Cummings and Lizabeth Scott, Paramount Pictures, 1945.

INTERVIEWS AND Q & A's

Interviews by Barbara and Nathaniel Branden, tape recording, New York, New York, December 1960–May 1961.

Interview by Johnny Carson, *The Tonight Show Starring Johnny Carson*, National Broadcasting Company, August 11, October 26, and December 13, 1967.

Interview by Phil Donahue, *Donahue*, WGN Chicago, April 29, 1980.

Interview by Jerry Schwartz, "Interview with Ayn Rand," *The Objectivist Forum*, June and August 1980.

Interview by Alvin Toffler, *Playboy* magazine, March 1964.

"Philosophy of Objectivism" lecture course, question periods, tape recording, New York, NY, 1976.

"Global Balkanization," Ford Hall Forum question period, tape recording, Boston, MA, April 10, 1977.

"Objective Communication" lecture course question period, tape recording, New York, NY 1980.

POSTHUMOUS PUBLICATIONS

The Art of Fiction, ed. Tore Boeckmann (New York: Penguin, 2000).

The Art of Nonfiction, ed. by Robert Mayhew (New York: Penguin, 2001).

The Ayn Rand Column, ed. by Peter Schwartz (New Milford, CT: Second Renaissance Books, 1998).

"Ayn Rand's Q & A's," ed. by Robert Mayhew, in preparation.

The Early Ayn Rand, ed. by Leonard Peikoff (New York: New American Library, 1984). Includes "Ideal," "Red Pawn" (synopsis only), and "Think Twice."

Journals of Ayn Rand, ed. by David Harriman (New York: Penguin, 1997).

Letters of Ayn Rand, ed. by Michael S. Berliner (New York: Penguin, 1995).

The Objectivism Research CD-ROM (Indianapolis: Oliver Computing, 2001). Contains almost all of Rand's fiction and nonfiction.

Russian Writings on Hollywood, ed. by Michael S. Berliner (Irvine, CA: Ayn Rand Institute Press,1999). Contains two of Rand's Soviet-era articles and her film diary.

The Voice of Reason, ed. by Leonard Peikoff (New York: New American Library, 1989).

SECONDARY

Berliner, Michael S. "Ayn Rand in Russia," ARI *Archive Annual*, vol. 4, 2003.

——, "Ayn Rand in Review," ARI *Archive Annual*, Vol. 3, 2000.

Binswanger, Harry, ed., *The Ayn Rand Lexicon* (New York: New American Library, 1986).

——, "Ayn Rand's Philosophic Achievement," *The Objectivist Forum*, June, August and October, 1982.

——, interview by Scott McConnell, tape recording, telephone, 1999– 2001, *Ayn Rand Archives*.

Branden, Barbara, "A Biographical Essay," in Nathaniel Branden, *Who is Ayn Rand?* (New York: Random House, 1962).

Britting, Jeff, "Ayn Rand, Communism and the Hollywood Blacklist" (participant, panel discussion on video tape, presented in conjunction with *Ayn Rand: The Fountainhead*, American Writers Series, C-SPAN, April, 2002).

—, "Ayn Rand, Hollywood and Integrity: Remarks on the Fiftieth Anniversary of the Film Release of *The Fountainhead*" (presented at the Lloyd E. Rigler Theatre at the Egyptian Theater, Hollywood, California, 1999). *Ayn Rand Archives.*

Champagne, Maurice, *The Mysterious Valley* (Lafayette, CO: Atlantean Press, 1994).

Garmong, Dina, "Ayn Rand's Correspondence: Russia and America" (paper presented at Lyceum Conference, Irvine, Calif., 1997).

Gotthelf, Allan, *On Ayn Rand* (Belmont, CA: Wadsworth, 2000).

Greene, Daniel, interview by Michael Paxton for *Ayn Rand: A Sense of Life*, tape recording, New York, New York, 1996. *Ayn Rand Archives.*

Lyons, Eugene, *The Red Decade: The Stalinist Penetration of America* (Indianapolis: Bobbs-Merrill, 1941).

Mann, Arline, interview by Michael Paxton for *Ayn Rand: A Sense of Life*, tape recording, New York, New York, 1996. *Ayn Rand Archives.*

Mayhew, Robert, ed., *Essays on "We the Living"* (Lanham, MD: Rowman & Littlefield, 2004).

McConnell, Scott, ed., "100 Voices: An Oral History of Ayn Rand," in preparation. Includes interviews of Fern Goldberg Brown, June Kurisu, Susan Ludel, Ilona Royce-Smithkin and Duncan Scott.

Paxton, Michael, *Ayn Rand: A Sense of Life* (Layton, UT: Gibbs Smith, 1998).

Peikoff, Leonard, interview by Harry Binswanger, tape recording. *Ayn Rand Archives.* ca. 1993.

——, interview by Richard Ralston, tape recording. *Ayn Rand Archives*, c. 1993.

——, "My Thirty Years With Ayn Rand," *The Objectivist Forum*, June 1987.

——, *The Ominous Parallels: The End of Freedom in America* (New York: Stein and Day, 1982).

——, *Objectivism: The Philosophy of Ayn Rand* (New York: Penguin, 1991).

Perrin, Vincent L., *Ayn Rand: First Description Bibliography* (Rockville, MD: Quill & Brush, 1990).

Sures, Mary Ann and Charles, *Facets of Ayn Rand: A Memoir* (Irvine, CA: ARI Press, 2001).

Vallliant, James S. *The Passion of Ayn Rand's Critics* ((Dallas, TX: Durban House Publishing, forthcoming 2005).

Volkov, Solomon, *St. Petersburg: A Cultural History*, trans. Antonina W. Bouis (New York: Free Press Paperbacks, 1997).

ARCHIVES AND COLLECTIONS

The Ayn Rand Institute, Irvine, California. Ayn Rand Papers, including Russian correspondence from her family. Ayn Rand Institute *Special Collections*.

Hoover Institution, Stanford, California. Roy Childs Papers.

Library of Congress, Washington D.C. *Ayn Rand Papers*, Manuscript Division.

Los Angeles Public Library, Los Angeles, California. Picture Collection.

Margaret Herrick Library of the Academy of Motion Picture Arts and Sciences, Beverly Hills, California. Special Collections: *The King of Kings* still collection and Hal Wallis Production Files.

New York Public Library for the Performing Arts, New York, New York. Billy Rose Theatre Collection. George Abbott miscellany.

St. Petersburg State University Library, St. Petersburg, Russia. Alisa Rosenbaum miscellany.

FILM

Ayn Rand: A Sense of Life, dir. Michael Paxton, AG Media Corporation Ltd., Hollywood, 1997.

Das Indische Grabmal, dir. Joe May, perf. Paul Richter and Mia May, Joe May Co., Germany, 1921.

The Fountainhead, dir. King Vidor, perf. Gary Cooper, Patricia Neal and Raymond Massey, Warner Bros., Hollywood, 1949.

In the Heat of the Night, dir. Norman Jewison, perf. Sidney Poitier and Rod Steiger, United Artists, Hollywood, 1967.

The King of Kings, dir. Cecil B. DeMille, perf. Joseph Schildkraut and H. B. Warner, DeMille Productions, Culver City, 1927.

Die Nibelungun: Siegfried, dir. Fritz Lang, perf. Paul Richter and Margarethe Schön, Decla-Bioscop AG, Berlin, 1924.

Noi Vivi and *Addio Kira*, dir. Goffredo Alessandrini, perf. Alida Valli, Rossano Brazzi and Fosco Giachetti, Scalera Films, Rome, 1942; rev. by Duncan Scott Productions and released as *We the Living*, 1986.

WEB SITE

For additional audio books, audio and video lectures and courses by and about Ayn Rand and Objectivism, consult the Web site of the Ayn Rand Institute: www.aynrand.org. To keep current on newly released materials and analyses, see the *Ayn Rand Archives Annual* at http://www.aynrand.org/archives/archives.html

List of Illustrations

Page 24—Ayn Rand Archives

Page 25, top—Ayn Rand Archives

Page 25, bottom—Ayn Rand Archives

Page 26, top—Ayn Rand Archives

Page 26, bottom—Courtesy of Alex Lebedev (Ayn Rand Archives)

Page 27, left—Ayn Rand Archives

Page 27, right—Ayn Rand Archives

Page 28, left—Ayn Rand Archives

Page 28, right—Ayn Rand Archives

Page 31, top—Ayn Rand Archives

Page 31, middle—Ayn Rand Archives

Page 31, bottom—Ayn Rand Archives

Page 32, left—Ayn Rand Archives

Page 32, right—Ayn Rand Archives

Page 33—Courtesy Fern Brown (Ayn Rand Archives)

Page 34, top—Ayn Rand Archives

Page 34, bottom—Ayn Rand Archives

Page 35—Ayn Rand Archives

Page 36—Times World Wide Photo, Courtesy of *The New York Times*

Page 37—Ayn Rand Archives

Page 38—Photograph by Melbourne Spurr (Ayn Rand Archives)

Page 39—Ayn Rand Archives

Page 43—Ayn Rand Archives

Page 45, left—Ayn Rand Archives

Page 45, right—Ayn Rand Archives

Page 46, top—Reprinted with the permission of Scribner, an imprint of Simon & Schuster Adult Publishing Group, from WE THE LIVING by Ayn Rand (Ayn Rand Archives)

Page 46, bottom—Ayn Rand Archives

Page 48—Ayn Rand Archives

Page 49—Photograph by Pach Bros. (Ayn Rand Archives)

Page 51, left—Ayn Rand Archives

Page 51, right—Ayn Rand Archives

Page 53—Ayn Rand Archives

Page 74, bottom—Ayn Rand Archives

Page 75—Ayn Rand Archives

Page 77—Courtesy of the Frank Lloyd Wright Foundation. The drawings of Frank Lloyd Wright are Copyright © 1962, 1988, 2004 The Frank Lloyd Wright Foundation, Scottsdale, AZ

Page 78, top—Ayn Rand Archives

Page 78, bottom—Ayn Rand Archives

Page 80, top—Courtesy of June Kurisu (Ayn Rand Archives)

Page 80, bottom—Ayn Rand Archives

Page 81—Ayn Rand Archives

Page 82—Ayn Rand Archives

Page 83—Ayn Rand Archives

Page 84—Ayn Rand Archives

Page 85—Ayn Rand Archives

Page 86—Photograph by Phyllis Cerf (Ayn Rand Archives)

Page 87—Ayn Rand Archives

Page 88—Ayn Rand Archives

Page 89, top—Ayn Rand Archives

Page 89, middle—Ayn Rand Archives

Page 89, bottom—Ayn Rand Archives

Page 90—Courtesy Daniel E. Greene (Ayn Rand Archives)

Page 93—The Metropolitan Museum of Art, Gift of the Chester Dale Collection, 1955. (55.5) Photography © 1986 The Metropolitan Museum of Art

Page 95—Ayn Rand Archives

Page 96, top—Ayn Rand Archives

Page 96, middle—Ayn Rand Archives

Page 96, bottom, left—Ayn Rand Archives

Page 96, bottom, right—Ayn Rand Archives

Page 97, top—Photograph by Lester Kraus (Ayn Rand Archives)

Page 97, bottom—Courtesy of Penguin Group (USA) Inc. (Ayn Rand Archives)

Page 98, top—Ayn Rand Archives

Page 98, bottom—Ayn Rand Archives

Page 99—Ayn Rand Archives

Page 100, top—Photograph by Jeff Burch. All rights reserved.